C000015528

JUMP START
JAVASCRIPT

BY ARA PEHLIVANIAN
& DON NGUYEN

Jump Start JavaScript

by Ara Pehlivanian and Don Nguyen

Copyright © 2013 SitePoint Pty. Ltd.

Product Manager: Simon Mackie   **English Editor**: Kelly Steele

Technical Editor: Colin J. Ihrig   **Cover Designer**: Alex Walker

Notice of Rights

All rights reserved. No part of this book may be reproduced, stored in a retrieval system or transmitted in any form or by any means, without the prior written permission of the publisher, except in the case of brief quotations embodied in critical articles or reviews.

Notice of Liability

The author and publisher have made every effort to ensure the accuracy of the information herein. However, the information contained in this book is sold without warranty, either express or implied. Neither the authors and SitePoint Pty. Ltd., nor its dealers or distributors will be held liable for any damages to be caused either directly or indirectly by the instructions contained in this book, or by the software or hardware products described herein.

Trademark Notice

Rather than indicating every occurrence of a trademarked name as such, this book uses the names only in an editorial fashion and to the benefit of the trademark owner with no intention of infringement of the trademark.

Published by SitePoint Pty. Ltd.

48 Cambridge Street Collingwood
VIC Australia 3066
Web: www.sitepoint.com
Email: business@sitepoint.com

ISBN 978-0-9873321-8-9 (print)

ISBN 978-0-9873321-9-6 (ebook)
Printed and bound in the United States of America

About Ara Pehlivanian

Ara Pehlivanian has been working on the web since 1997. Most recently, he's worked on high-end, highly visible projects as a web developer and practice lead at Nurun, a front-end engineer at Yahoo! Mail and is currently a JavaScript developer on the HP Cloud Services team.

About Don Nguyen

Like many programmers, Don dabbled in JavaScript for a number years as a secondary language. It wasn't until he began implementing server-side projects in Node.js that JavaScript began to take center stage. Having been heavily involved in a number of web projects from the back-end all the way to the front, he is now equally at home with JavaScript on the client and on the server. He currently spends his time working on building startups from his home base of Sydney, Australia.

About SitePoint

SitePoint specializes in publishing fun, practical, and easy-to-understand content for web professionals. Visit http://www.sitepoint.com/ to access our blogs, books, newsletters, articles, and community forums. You'll find a stack of information on JavaScript, PHP, Ruby, mobile development, design, and more.

About Jump Start

Jump Start books provide you with a rapid and practical introduction to web development languages and technologies. Typically around 150 pages in length, they can be read in a weekend, giving you a solid grounding in the topic and the confidence to experiment on your own.

To my loving wife Krista, without whose grace, patience and support I would not have been able to write this; and to our two brilliant daughters.

—Ara

To Lorraine, thank you for keeping me nourished with hot food, a warm heart and a beaming smile.

—Don

Table of Contents

Chapter 6   **The Document Object Model** 101

Preface

JavaScript is a very powerful, versatile, and ubiquitous programming language. From humble beginnings[1] in the mid-1990s as Netscape's foil to Microsoft's Visual Basic, it's grown to be one of the world's most popular[2] programming languages.

JavaScript is unique among programming languages because it's the only one deployed on practically all personal computers around the world. All modern web browsers implement JavaScript. It's the de facto scripting language for the Web. While it started out as a simple language used for validating forms and minimally manipulating some content in the page, it's evolved to let you build rich client-side applications. What's more, over the years, JavaScript has even begun to supplant Flash to some degree.

As the Web continues to grow and evolve, the need for JavaScript developers is increasing. Whether you're an experienced programmer looking to pick up JavaScript, or a novice wanting to fill some of that demand, this book will help you. After reading this book you should be able to write your own JavaScript applications and have enough of an understanding of the language to get you started down the road to becoming an expert JavaScript developer.

Who Should Read This Book

Web designers and developers wanting to get up to speed with JavaScript quickly. Knowledge of HTML and CSS is assumed.

Conventions Used

You'll notice that we've used certain typographic and layout styles throughout this book to signify different types of information. Look out for the following items.

Code Samples

Code in this book will be displayed using a fixed-width font, like so:

---

[1] http://en.wikipedia.org/wiki/JavaScript#Birth_at_Netscape
[2] http://javascript.crockford.com/javascript.html

```
<h1>A Perfect Summer's Day</h1>
<p>It was a lovely day for a walk in the park. The birds
were singing and the kids were all back at school.</p>
```

If the code is to be found in the book's code archive, the name of the file will appear at the top of the program listing, like this:

```
                                                        example.css
.footer {
  background-color: #CCC;
  border-top: 1px solid #333;
}
```

If only part of the file is displayed, this is indicated by the word *excerpt*:

```
                                                  example.css (excerpt)
  border-top: 1px solid #333;
```

If additional code is to be inserted into an existing example, the new code will be displayed in bold:

```
function animate() {
  new_variable = "Hello";
}
```

Also, where existing code is required for context, rather than repeat all the code, a ⋮ will be displayed:

```
function animate() {
  ⋮
  return new_variable;
}
```

Some lines of code are intended to be entered on one line, but we've had to wrap them because of page constraints. A ➥ indicates a line break that exists for formatting purposes only, and should be ignored.

```
URL.open("http://www.sitepoint.com/responsive-web-design-real-user-
➥testing/?responsive1");
```

Tips, Notes, and Warnings

 ### Hey, You!

Tips will give you helpful little pointers.

 ### Ahem, Excuse Me ...

Notes are useful asides that are related—but not critical—to the topic at hand. Think of them as extra tidbits of information.

 ### Make Sure You Always ...

... pay attention to these important points.

 ### Watch Out!

Warnings will highlight any gotchas that are likely to trip you up along the way.

Supplementary Materials

http://www.sitepoint.com/books/jsjavascript1/
The book's website, containing links, updates, resources, and more.

http://www.sitepoint.com/books/jsjavascript1/code.php
The downloadable code archive for this book.

http://www.sitepoint.com/forums/forumdisplay.php?15-JavaScript-amp-jQuery
SitePoint's forums, for help on any tricky web problems.

books@sitepoint.com
Our email address, should you need to contact us for support, to report a problem, or for any other reason.

Do you want to keep learning?

Thanks for buying this book. We appreciate your support. Do you want to continue learning? You can now get unlimited access to courses and ALL SitePoint books at Learnable for one low price. Enroll now and start learning today! Join Learnable and you'll stay ahead of the newest technology trends: http://www.learnable.com.

Once you've mastered the principles of JavaScript, challenge yourself with our online quiz. Can you achieve a perfect score? Head on over to http://quizpoint.com/#categories/JAVASCRIPT.

Setting Up

As a JavaScript developer, you'll be writing code that runs in the browser. And as we walk through the book, you *could* create an HTML document in which you'd add your JavaScript code, but it will be a little while yet before we tackle a full project, and you'll want to test things out in the meantime. The best way is to jump right in by opening up your browser's console and typing the examples in there. All the major browser vendors have a console, and there are instructions below on how to activate it in each. Once you have the console open, you'll find a prompt next to which you can click and start typing. In most consoles, it looks like an angle bracket: >. In Internet Explorer, the prompt is two angle brackets: >>.

 Spinning a Line

When you need a new line within the console, rather than pressing **Enter**, which will execute the code, press **Shift Enter** for a new line.

Console

This section describes how to reach the developer console in several of today's most popular browsers. If your browser of choice is not covered here, a quick Google search will be sure to turn up the results you need.

Chrome

To activate Chrome's Developer Tools in Windows and Linux, press **Control Shift J**. On Mac, press **⌥⌘J (option command J)**. This will open the console tab in the Developer Tools' panel, which is where we want to be, as seen in Figure 1.1.

Figure 1.1. Console in Chrome

Firefox

To activate Firefox's Web Console in Windows and Linux, press **Control Shift K**. On Mac, press **⌥⌘K (option command K)**. The result is shown in Figure 1.2.

Figure 1.2. The Web Console in Firefox

Internet Explorer

To activate Internet Explorer's Developer Tools panel, presented in Figure 1.3, press **F12**.

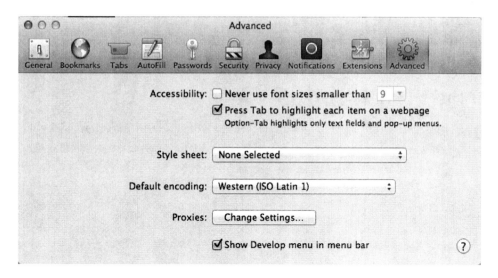

Figure 1.3. Developer Tools in Internet Explorer

Safari

Activating the console in Safari is a bit more involved than in other browsers. First, you need to enable the **Develop** menu in the menu bar. To do that, enter Safari's settings by pressing ⌘, **(command comma)**, going to the **Advanced** tab, and checking the **Show Develop menu in menu bar** checkbox, as shown in Figure 1.4.

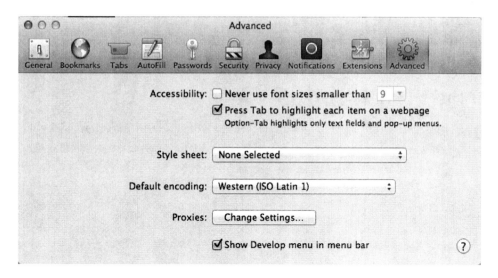

Figure 1.4. Enabling the **Develop** menu

Once you've done that, close the options window and then press ⌥⌘C **(option command C)** to bring up the console, seen in Figure 1.5.

Figure 1.5. Console in Safari

Using JavaScript in HTML Files

If you'd prefer to skip the console and work inside an HTML document, you could go about it in one of two ways: you could write the code directly in the HTML document, or write it in a separate JavaScript file and load it up from the HTML file.

In the HTML File

HTML provides a `<script>` tag, inside of which you can write executable JavaScript code. Here's an example of a very simple HTML document with one line of JavaScript that pops up an alert dialog with the message, `Hello, world!`:

js-in-html.html

```html
<!doctype html>
<html>
  <head>
    <title>Code inside an HTML document</title>
    <script>
      alert("Hello, world!");
    </script>
  </head>
  <body>
  </body>
</html>
```

In a Separate File

You can also place the code in a separate file and link to it. So, for example, we could place our `alert` statement inside a file we name **hello.js** (the **.js** file extension indicates that this is a JavaScript source file) and then link to it using the `<script>` tag's `src` attribute like so:

external-js.html

```
<!doctype html>
<html>
  <head>
    <title>Code inside an HTML document</title>
    <script src="hello.js"></script>
  </head>
  <body>
  </body>
</html>
```

Note that you cannot have a self-closing `<script>` tag. In other words, the following will fail to work:

```
<!-- This won't work -->
<script src="hello.js" />
```

You must include both the start and end tags, even if there is nothing inside them, as shown below:

```
<script src="hello.js"></script>
```

Location of the `<script>` Tag

We'll be covering the DOM in detail later, but for now it's important to know that when the browser reads an HTML document, it converts the tags it encounters into an internal representation called the **Document Object Model**, or DOM. You can then write JavaScript that interacts with your HTML via manipulation of the DOM. Be aware that if you try to access the DOM before the browser has had a chance to finish building it, you'll receive errors.

When you include a `<script>` tag in the document's head, the code within it will execute right away, even if the DOM is yet to be built. So, any reference to DOM elements will result in an error since the HTML inside the `<body>` isn't there yet. There are two ways to deal with this. You can wrap your code in the document's `onload` function, which the browser executes once it's done constructing the DOM. Alternatively, you could include your script tag(s) at the very end of the document's body, immediately before the closing `</body>` tag.

The latter is the preferred method because when the browser constructs the DOM, it fires off requests to the server for every `<img>` tag it encounters. It won't call `onload` until all the images have finished loading. This means that any JavaScript you'd like to run on the page will have to wait until all the page's images and other resources are done loading. This may be insignificant on pages with just a bit of text and an image or two. But, on pages with lots of images, you'll have a noticeable delay before your scripts execute. Therefore, it's better to place your scripts at the end of the document's body.

Here's an HTML document that includes embedded JavaScript as well as a reference to an external JavaScript file. Though the code in the document's head references nothing in the DOM, (it's a simple `alert` statement), it will only execute once the scripts have loaded at the end of the document:

```html
<!doctype html>
<html>
  <head>
    <title>Code inside an HTML document</title>
    <script>
      window.onload = function () {
        alert("Hello, world!");
      };
    </script>
  </head>
  <body>
    <h1>An example</h1>
    <p>Here's an example document with loads of images.</p>
    <ul>
      <li><img src="pic1.jpg" /></li>
      <li><img src="pic2.jpg" /></li>
      <li><img src="pic3.jpg" /></li>
      <!-- lots more -->
    </ul>
    <script src="hello.js"></script>
    <script src="another.js"></script>
```

```
    <script src="and-another.js"></script>
  </body>
</html>
```

Summary

After reading this chapter, you should be ready to jump into the world of JavaScript development. This chapter has shown you how to work with JavaScript in your browser of choice. You've also learned the various methods for incorporating JavaScript into web pages. Now that you're set up, the rest of the book will focus on the fundamentals of the JavaScript language.

Chapter 7

Variables

Programming is basically the manipulation of data. In order to manipulate it, though, we first need to store it somewhere. In JavaScript, variables are the most basic form of data storage. Just like in algebra, variables are representatives of information we want to work with. Unlike algebra, though, there's no restriction to only using letters. We can use whole words to more accurately describe what we're dealing with, such as `name`, `tax`, `length`, or `width`. We can also use multiple words combined together, like `firstName`, `taskList`, or `timeToLive`. Notice that the first word in each multi-word variable name is all lowercase, while the first letter of each subsequent word is capitalized. This is known as **camel casing**, and it is the naming convention used in the JavaScript community.

First, a Quick Comment

You'll be seeing a lot of comments throughout the code examples in this book, so it's best to explain what they are here. **Comments** are bits of nonexecuting text that can be inserted into code to describe what's going on. In JavaScript, comments come in two forms, single-line comments and multi-line comments. Single-line comments are indicated by two forward slashes (//). Anything that follows the double slashes of a single-line comment is considered nonexecuting text, but only until the end of that line. On the other hand, multi-line (or block) comments can span multiple lines. Multi-line comments begin with a slash star combination (/*) and continue until a star slash (*/) combination is encountered.

Here are some examples of single-line comments:

```
// I'm about to declare a variable and give it a value
var myVariable = "Hello, world."; // Just did it!
```

And here's a multi-line comment:

```
/* I just declared a variable named myVariable and assigned
   the value "Hello, world." to it. I preceded it with a
   comment stating that I was about to do just that, and then
   followed it with another comment on the same line stating
   that I just did it. I'm now writing a really long comment
   that needs more than one line, so I've made this one a
   multiline comment.
*/
```

Declarations

Declaring a variable is simple enough:

```
var task = "Write the first chapter.";
```

Here, we've declared a variable named task using a variable declaration statement. Using the var keyword, you can declare one or more variables and optionally initialize them with a value. So, for example:

```
var task = "Write the first chapter.",
    complete = true;
```

We've declared two variables (separated by a comma), and assigned a string to the first and a Boolean value to the second (there's more on variable types, such as string and Boolean, shortly). Note how we're only using one declaration statement to declare and initialize both variables. You can also use multiple declaration statements—one for each variable declaration.

A Sensitive Issue

JavaScript is a case-sensitive language, so `task` and `Task` are treated as entirely different variables. Likewise, when we look at naming functions later on, case sensitivity will be important. Just remember to always use the same case when referring to a variable.

Terminate Each Line

The semicolon at the end of the line tells JavaScript that this line of code is complete. If you leave it out, JavaScript will attempt to insert a semicolon when it's reading your code. This is known as automatic semicolon insertion. As a general guideline, you shouldn't leave your program's functionality to guesswork. It's best to be sure and terminate each line with a semicolon.

One last point about variable declaration and initialization: It's best to keep the two separate. It's common to run into trouble when using a debugger to walk through code. When variables are declared and initialized in the same statement, the debugger skips over the whole line in one step. If there's any trouble with one of the initializations, you won't be able to examine each assignment individually. Instead, it's better to declare all your variables together and initialize them all separately, like so:

```
// declaration
var task, complete;

// initialization
task = "Write the first chapter.";
complete = true;
```

Later, we'll see how it's possible to perform calculations and operations during value assignment. We'll also see how doing so can make debugging more difficult.

Saving Space

Some examples in this book may go against this rule, declaring and initializing variables in a single statement. This is usually done in order to save page space.

Types

If you've had any exposure to programming languages like C or Java, you've likely noticed that there was no specification that we wanted `task` to hold a string (as opposed to a Boolean or numeric value). This is because JavaScript is a **loosely typed language**, unlike C or Java, which are strongly typed. This means that even though JavaScript does recognize types internally, you don't need to explicitly declare a variable to be of a certain type. You can also change a variable's type on the fly. JavaScript tries to figure out what you're trying to do with your variables instead of relying on you to explicitly say it. In fact, there's no way to tell JavaScript that you want your variable to be of a certain type, apart from assigning a value of that type to the variable.

There are six data types you can work with: **number**, **string**, **Boolean**, **null**, **undefined**, and **object**.

Number

Unlike in other languages, the only numeric type JavaScript has is `Number`. According to the ECMAScript standard[1], `Number` holds a double-precision 64-bit binary format IEEE 754 value. `Number` can hold a set of all possible `Number` values including the special Not-a-Number (`NaN`) values, positive infinity, and negative infinity.

 When Is a Number Not a Number?

Not-a-Number or `NaN` is a special value that's returned by JavaScript when math functions fail (`Math.abs("foo")`), or when a function trying to parse a number fails (`Number("foo")`). `NaN` is special because it's the only value in JavaScript that doesn't equal itself. In other words, both `NaN == NaN` and `NaN === NaN` return `false` when logically you'd expect them to be `true` since `NaN` is `NaN`. However, true to its meaning `NaN` itself is "not a number" and therefore is not equal to itself.

There is an `isNaN` function to verify if a returned value is actually `NaN`. but be careful, because the results can be confusing. The reason is that `isNaN` first tries to convert the value that you pass it into a number through a process called type conversion (which we'll cover later) and, as a result, some values convert into

---

[1] http://www.ecma-international.org/publications/standards/Ecma-262.htm

numbers while others don't. For example, it will return `true` for `isNaN(NaN)`, `undefined`, and an object literal (`{}`)—they are all not numbers. It will not, however, return `true` for values of `true` and `null`, which are also not numbers.

Where it becomes even trickier is in dealing with strings. It will return `false` for numbers in strings such as `isNaN("42")`, since `"42"` is converted to 42, which is a number. It will also return `false` for empty strings (`""`) and strings consisting only of spaces (`"  "`) since they'll convert to 0, which is also a number. But strings with text in them that fail when parsed as a number (like `isNaN("foo")`) will return NaN. So, even though `"foo"` is clearly not equal to NaN, it returns `true` when you pass it into `isNaN`.

The only truly reliable way to test for whether a value is actually NaN is to compare it against itself. Since NaN is the sole value that doesn't equal itself, it will return `false` and you'll know that what you're dealing with is in fact NaN.

String

Strings holds all possible string values. Some examples include:

```
"Hello, world!"
"1, 2, 3, 4, 5"
"!@#$%^&*()_+"
```

Boolean

Boolean variables can only hold the values `true` or `false`.

Undefined

Undefined is an odd data type because it represents the state of a variable that's been declared but without a value assigned to it. By definition, though, the fact that the variable exists means that it's defined, which is what makes this data type unusual.

Null

Null is used when you want to declare a variable and intentionally express the absence of a value (unlike `undefined` where the value is simply absent).

Object

An object is a collection of properties. The properties can be any of the previously mentioned types, as well as other objects and functions (which we'll cover later).

Operations

Having data is great, but doing something with it is better. You may have a couple of strings that you want to concatenate, or a few numbers you'd like to do some math with. Well, it's fairly straightforward to perform these tasks using JavaScript. Concatenating strings is as easy as using the + symbol:

```
var fname, lname, fullName;

fname = "John";
lname = "Doe";
fullName = fname + " " + lname; // fullName is "John Doe"
```

Math operations are carried out as you'd expect, using the addition (+), subtraction (-), multiplication (*), division (/), and modulus (%) operators:

```
var widgets, gizmos, inventory;

widgets = 1043;
gizmos = 2279;
inventory = widgets + gizmos; // inventory is 3322
```

Similarly:

```
var provincial, federal, subtotal, total;

provincial = 0.095;
federal = 0.05;
subtotal = 10;
total = subtotal + (subtotal * provincial)
➥ + (subtotal * federal); // total is 11.45
```

Finally, you can use the remainder (%) operator to end up with just the remainder of a division returned to you. So, for example, 10 % 3 will return 1.

The Dangers of Loose Typing

Although JavaScript does its best to figure out what you're doing with your variables, and has no requirement for strong typing, it's important to consider the type of data your variables will be holding; otherwise, you may run into some problems.

For example, consider:

```
var johnTaskCount = 11,
    janeTaskCount = "42",
    totalTaskCount = johnTaskCount + janeTaskCount;
```

At a glance, John has 11 tasks and Jane has 42, which should total 53 tasks. However, since the value of janeTaskCount is a string, JavaScript sees the plus symbol on the third line as an attempted concatenation instead of an addition. The result is "1142" instead of the expected number, 53.

For the right result, we have to ensure that both variables hold actual numbers and not strings, like this:

```
var johnTaskCount = 11,
    janeTaskCount = 42,
    totalTaskCount = johnTaskCount + janeTaskCount;
```

Type Conversion (aka Type Coercion)

When JavaScript is given an operation involving conflicting variable types, it tries to normalize them first before performing the operation. This is the case in arithmetic or string operations (as shown) or comparisons (which we'll cover in a moment). Because you can't add a word to a number, it first converts the number to a string and then concatenates the two (as we saw a moment ago). Likewise, if you attempt to add a number to a Boolean (true or false), it will first convert the Boolean to its numeric representation—1 for true and 0 for false—and then add that to the number. This is a very important aspect of the language to understand, as not knowing about it could lead to unintended errors cropping up in your programs.

Comparison Operators

Comparison operators compare two values and return either `true` or `false` based on how they compare. So, if we want to know whether 10 is greater than 5, we'd write 10 > 5 and that comparison would return `true`. However, 10 > 11 would return `false`.

Equal (==)

Equal returns `true` if both values are equal. If the values being compared are not of the same type, JavaScript first converts them and then applies a strict comparison. So, if the values are a number and a Boolean, they'll be converted to numbers before the comparison. If a string is involved, both values are converted to strings before comparing. If they're objects, they're equal if both values are referring to the same location in memory:

```
1 == 1      // returns true
"1" == 1    // returns true ("1" converts to 1)
1 == true   // returns true
0 == false  // returns true
"" == 0     // returns true ("" converts to 0)
"  " == 0   // returns true ("  " converts to 0)

0 == 1      // returns false
1 == false  // returns false
0 == true   // returns false

var x, y;   // declare x and y
x = {};     // create an object and assign it to x
y = x;      // point y to x
x == y;     // returns true (refers to same object in memory)
x == {};    // returns false (not the same object)
```

Not Equal (!=)

This is the same as equal, but it works in reverse: `true` is returned if the values are not equal. The same conversions described above apply here as well:

```
1 != 1      // returns false
"1" != 1    // returns false ("1" converts to 1)
1 != true   // returns false
```

```
0 != false // returns false
"" != 0    // returns false ("" converts to 0)
"  " != 0  // returns false ("  " converts to 0)

0 != 1     // returns true
1 != false // returns true
0 != true  // returns true

var x, y;  // declare x and y
x = {};    // create an object and assign it to x
y = x;     // point y to x
x != y;    // returns false (refers to same object in memory)
x != {};   // returns true (not the same object)
```

Strict Equal (===)

A strict equal comparison performs no conversion of types. Where `" "` `==` 0 would return true for a regular equal comparison, `" "` `===` 0 would not, since an empty string does not equal zero:

```
1 === 1    // returns true

"1" === 1  // returns false ("1" is not converted)
1 === true // returns false
0 === false // returns false
"" === 0   // returns false ("" is not converted)
"  " === 0 // returns false ("  " is not converted)
0 === 1    // returns false
1 === false // returns false
0 === true // returns false

var x, y;  // declare x and y
x = {};    // create an object and assign it to x
y = x;     // point y to x
x === y;   // returns true (refers to same object in memory)
x === {};  // returns false (not the same object)
```

Strict Not Equal (!==)

Strict not equal is the samle as strict equal except that it works in reverse. It returns true if the values are not equal. Again, no conversions are performed prior to comparison:

```
1 !== 1       // returns false

"1" !== 1     // returns true ("1" is not converted)
1 !== true    // returns true
0 !== false   // returns true
"" !== 0      // returns true ("" is not converted)
"  " !== 0    // returns true ("  " is not converted)
0 !== 1       // returns true
1 !== false   // returns true
0 !== true    // returns true

var x, y;     // declare x and y
x = {};       // create an object and assign it to x
y = x;        // point y to x
x !== y;      // returns false (refers to same object in memory)
x !== {};     // returns true (not the same object)
```

Greater than (>)

Greater than returns true if the value on the left of the operator is greater than the value on the right. Note that type conversion implicitly occurs before comparison:

```
0 > 1  // returns false
1 > 1  // returns false
2 > 1  // returns true
2 > "" // returns true ("" converts to 0)
```

Greater than or Equal to (>=)

This returns true if the value on the left is greater than or equal to the one on the right. Note that type conversion implicitly occurs before comparison:

```
0 >= 1   // returns false
1 >= 1   // returns true
"1" >= 1 // returns true ("1" converts to 1)
```

Less than (<)

This returns true if the value on the left of the operator is less than the value on the right. Note that type conversion implicitly occurs before comparison:

```
0 < 1 // returns true
1 < 1 // returns false
2 < 1 // returns false
2 < "" // returns false ("" converts to 0)
```

Less than or Equal to (<=)

This returns `true` if the value on the left of the operator is less than or equal to the value on the right. Note that type conversion implicitly occurs before comparison:

```
0 <= 1   // returns true
1 <= 1   // returns true
"1" <= 1 // returns true ("1" converts to 1)
2 <= 1   // returns false
"2" <= 1 // returns false ("2" converts to 2)
```

Logic Flow

Now that we've covered comparison operators, we can use them to control the logic flow of our programs. Sometimes your program will need to execute different code under different conditions. For example, if the time is before noon, we should display a "Good Morning!" message, but if it's later in the day, "Good Afternoon!" or even "Good Evening!" would be more appropriate. The way to do this is to use the `if...else` statement to evaluate conditions and fork code execution.

Figure 2.1 shows how logic flow can be controlled through comparison statements. If a condition is met, the code branches in a given direction. If not, it falls to the next condition. In our flow diagram, we assume a time of 1900 hours or 7 PM. We then check it against various time ranges to see where it falls. So, if the time value is greater than or equal to 0000 (midnight) and less than 1200 (noon), we set our message to "Good morning!". If it's greater than or equal to 1200 and less than 1700 (5 PM), we set the message to "Good afternoon!". We continue this pattern until we've checked every range leading us to midnight.

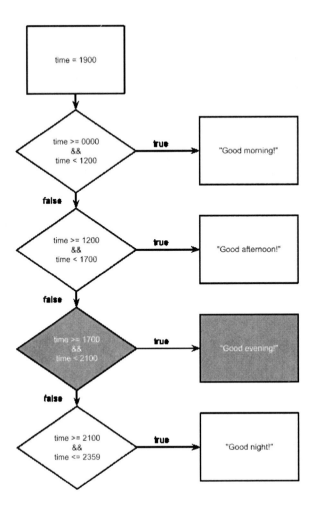

Figure 2.1. Logic flow

&& symbols

You'll notice the use of **&&** symbols in Figure 2.1. This is a logical AND operator. Along with it, there's also the logical OR (**||**) as well as the logical NOT (**!**). The AND and OR operators convert values to Boolean values and then return one of the two. The NOT operator inverses the Boolean value of an operand. Here are a few examples of the logical AND operator. Notice how if the first of the two values evaluates to `false`, it is returned; otherwise, the second value is returned:

```
true && true;   // returns true
true && false;  // returns false
false && true;  // returns false
0 && 1;         // returns 0
0 && 2;         // returns 0
1 && 0;         // returns 0
2 && 0;         // returns 0
"foo" && "bar"  // returns "bar"
```

Here are a few examples of the logical OR operator. Note how if the first of the two values evaluates to **true**, it is returned; otherwise, the second value is returned:

```
true || true;    // returns true
true || false;   // returns true
false || true;   // returns true
0 || 1;          // returns 1
0 || 2;          // returns 2
1 || 0;          // returns 1
2 || 0;          // returns 2
"foo" || "bar";  // returns foo
```

Here are a few examples of the logical NOT operator. Note how it inverts the Boolean value of the operand:

```
!true;   // returns false
!false;  // returns true
!0;      // returns true
!1;      // returns false
!"foo";  // returns false
```

Let's write some code that does what's represented in Figure 2.1:

time-of-day.html (excerpt)

```
var d, hours, minutes, time, message;

// Get the current time's hour and minute components
d = new Date();
hours = d.getHours();
minutes = d.getMinutes();
```

```
// Make sure the hour is a double digit string
if (hours < 10) {
  hours = "0" + hours; // converts hours to string
} else {
  hours = hours.toString();
}

// Make sure the minutes are a double digit string
if (minutes < 10) {
  minutes = "0" + minutes; // converts minutes to string
} else {
  minutes = minutes.toString();
}

// Concatenate hours and minutes into a quadruple digit number
// representing the time in 24 hour format
time = Number(hours + minutes);

if (time >= 0000 && time < 1200) {
  message = "Good morning!";
} else if (time >= 1200 && time < 1700) {
  message = "Good afternoon!";
} else if (time >= 1700 && time < 2100) {
  message = "Good evening!";
} else if (time >= 2100 && time <= 2359) {
  message = "Good night!";
}

alert(message);
```

In this example, we establish the current time by instantiating a new Date object and reading the hours and minutes values from it. The Date object is set to the date and time at the moment it was instantiated. Now, since we need a four-digit number to represent our time of day, and since hours and minutes can be in the single digits (if it's two minutes past the hour, the minutes will be 2, not 02), we need to pad the values. We check to see if the values we're given are less than 10. If so, we pad them with a zero. By doing this, we're actually accomplishing two tasks at once. By adding a "0" string to our digit rather than a numeric 0 (which would do nothing), we're triggering type coercion and turning our digit into a string. If, however, our hours or minutes value is in the double-digits, we only convert it to a string by calling the toString method.

Once we have both the `hours` and `minutes` values, we concatenate them to receive a nice four-digit representation, and then we convert it back to a number from a string. That way, as a number, we can use comparison operators to check the current time against our ranges. Notice how we've already used the `if...else` syntax to prepare our `hours` and `minutes` values? We use it again to compare our time value against values we've set to determine when morning, afternoon, evening, and night are. When one of the clauses are met (in the case of our example, it's when the 1900 falls between 1700 and 2100), we set the value of `message` to `"Good evening!"` and then alert the user, as seen in Figure 2.2.

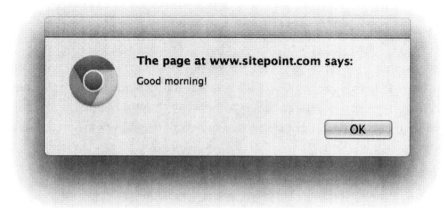

Figure 2.2. Logic flow output

Shortening Code With The Ternary Operator

Sometimes, if you want to avoid having a verbose `if...else` statement in your code, you can shorten it by using the ternary operator. Here's the way it's structured: `condition ? expression1 : expression2`. So we could write the first `if...else` in the previous example like this instead:

```
hours = (hours < 10) ? "0" + hours : hours.toString();
```

Sometimes, this syntax makes it easier and cleaner to read your code. Sometimes it doesn't. Use your judgment and pick the one that's easiest to understand what's going on.

Project

In order to tie together what we're learning, we're going to build a project as we go through this book: a task manager. For now, let's populate some variables with tasks:

```
                                                                    project.js
var task1, task2, task3;

task1 = "Pay phone bill";
task2 = "Write best-selling novel";
task3 = "Walk the dog";
```

Summary

In this chapter, we covered variables, data types, operators, and basic control flow. These are the the building blocks of all JavaScript programs. If any of this material is still unclear to you, please go back and read the chapter again. It is absolutely critical that you understand how these basics work before moving on to more complex topics.

Chapter **3**

Arrays

We saw in Chapter 2 how variables store different types of data. But in the case of something like a to-do list, where you have more than one item to deal with, you're going to need a way to store a collection of data. This is where arrays come in.

Creating an Array

You can create an array in a couple of ways:

```
var myArray = new Array();
```

Or:

```
var myArray = [];
```

The [ ] notation is called an **array literal**, and it represents an empty array. It's less verbose and safer to use than the new Array() syntax, because the Array constructor can be overwritten and potentially replaced with malicious code; for example, a function that masquerades as an array but sends any data you place in it to a third-party server on the Internet. Using the array literal, you can easily create a new array containing values such as the following:

```
var myArray = [4, 8, 15, 16, 23, 42];
```

An array isn't limited to numbers, though. You can also create an array with strings in it:

```
var fruit = ["apple", "orange", "pear", "grapes"];
```

Furthermore, you can mix the types of data stored in the array:

```
var stuff = [1, "apple", undefined, 42, "tanks", null, []];
```

Adding to an Array

There's no need to pre-populate an array with data, though. You can create an empty array and then add data to it later in several ways. One way is by index:

```
var myArray = [];

myArray[0] = "Hello";
myArray[1] = "World";
```

The contents of this array are now: ["Hello", "World"]. By specifying 0 in the square brackets, we're telling JavaScript that we want the value stored at index 0. In this example, the string "Hello" is assigned to the zeroth position. Similarly, the string "World" is stored at index one. Figure 3.1 shows how this looks.

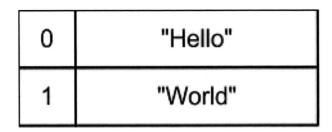

Figure 3.1. An array with indices

Speaking of indices, it's important to remember that array indices are zero-based. This means that the first item is stored at position 0, the second at position 1, the third at position 2, and so on. It can cause confusion, however, and lead to one-off errors. For example, you might ask for the item at index one and expect the first array element, but, in reality, you'd be accessing the second element.

It's also possible to use named indices:

```
var myArray = [];

myArray["fruit"] = "apple";
myArray["vehicle"] = "tank";
```

This creates an **associative array** where items are stored by a named index rather than a numbered index. However, we'd discourage the use of associative arrays. The preferred way to store data with named indices is by using objects, which we'll discuss in the next chapter.

As mentioned earlier, there are a couple of ways to add data to an array. The second approach is to use the push method. This is useful in situations where you wish to add items to the end of an array, but want to avoid calculating the index required to access the final position. Instead, you can do this:

```
myArray.push("hello");
```

By using push, you simply add a new item to the existing array. If it's an empty array, the data is written to position 0. If there are ten items in the array, the data is written to position 10 (remember, indices are zero-based).

Reading from an Array

Reading from an array is fairly straightforward. All you need to do is point to the item you want by its index number and the array will return it to you, like so:

```
var myValue,
    myArray = ["Hello", "World", "I", "am", "an", "array"];

myValue = myArray[4]; // returns "an"
```

Here we have an array containing six items. Since arrays are zero-indexed, the word
"Hello" resides at position 0, "World" is at 1, "I" is at 2, and so on. By passing the
index 4 to myArray, we're requesting the fifth item in the array, which is the word
"an".

Nested Arrays

Sometimes, you'll need to store an array within an array. Sometimes, you'll require
even more nesting. A quick warning: although it's possible to nest a number of arrays,
we advise against it, as working with many array indices can be confusing.

Let's start with two simple arrays, which we'll call yusuf and dreamers. We'll fill
dreamers with some values:

```
var yusuf, dreamers;

yusuf = [];
dreamers = ["cobb", "arthur", "ariadne", "saito", "fischer"];
```

Now, reading any of the values from the dreamers array is as simple as passing in
an index, which means placing the index value between a set of square brackets
placed next to the array name. So, if we wanted "cobb", we'd pass in an index of
0:

```
var dreamer = dreamers[0]; // returns "cobb"
```

But what if dreamers wasn't a named array but merely defined inline:

```
var yusuf;

yusuf = [["cobb", "arthur", "ariadne", "saito", "fischer"]];
```

How would we now get to "cobb"? By using: yusuf[0][0]. In the first square
brackets, we'd define the index of the first array we want to read from; in the second
set, we'd define the second index. So, reading "arthur" would be yusuf[0][1],
"ariadne" would be yusuf[0][2], and so on.

Let's take it a bit further:

```
var reality = ["yusuf", ["arthur", ["eames", ["cobb", "ariadne",
➥"saito", "fischer"]]]];
```

Here, we have an outer array called `reality`. It contains the string `"yusuf"` and a nested array. The nested array contains the string `"arthur"` and another nested array, and so on. Reading values from this nested set would be as follows:

```
reality[0];               // returns "yusuf"
reality[1][0];            // returns "arthur"
reality[1][1][0];         // returns "eames"
reality[1][1][1][0];      // returns "cobb"
reality[1][1][1][1];      // returns "ariadne"
reality[1][1][1][2];      // returns "saito"
reality[1][1][1][3];      // returns "fischer"
```

As you can see, keeping track of matters can become complicated, especially when each array contains several items—several of which are arrays themselves.

What can you do with arrays?

Now that we've covered the basics of an array and how data is stored in them, let's look at what you can do with arrays. There are seven mutator methods that let you modify the contents of the array: `pop`, `push`, `reverse`, `shift`, `sort`, `splice`, and `unshift`. There are also four widely supported accessor methods that don't modify the array but allow you to access its contents in different ways: `concat`, `join`, `slice`, and `toString`.

 On Browser Support

Since JavaScript support varies from browser to browser and from browser version to browser version, there are varying degrees of support to contend with. For example, browsers implementing JavaScript 1.6 and higher also support the `indexOf` and `lastIndexOf` accessor methods. They'll also support the following iteration methods: `forEach`, `every`, `some`, `filter`, and `map`. Finally, browsers supporting JavaScript 1.8 or higher will also support the `reduce` and `reduceRight` iteration methods.

It used to be that browser makers released a new version of their product once every few months or even years. Nowadays, though, they're doing it much faster—at least Google and Mozilla are with Chrome and Firefox. To give you an example, while Internet Explorer is at version 10 and Safari at version 6 as of this writing, Firefox and Chrome are at versions 21 and 28 respectively. With new versions coming out so quickly (and updates being made transparently with the browser updating itself whenever you restart it), it's very difficult to pin down which version supports what functionality, especially in print. If you need to know which version of what browser supports a particular feature you want to use, you can utilize a tool like http://caniuse.com/. Type in a method name and you'll be given a table of all the supporting browsers, their versions, and how well the feature is implemented.

Mutator Methods

pop

pop will remove the last element from the array and return it to you:

```
var tasks = [
  "Pay phone bill",
  "Write best-selling novel",
  "Walk the dog"
];

tasks.pop(); // returns "Walk the dog"
```

push

push will add an item to the end of the array and return the array's new length:

```
var tasks = [
  "Pay phone bill",
  "Write best-selling novel",
  "Walk the dog"
];

tasks.push("Feed the cat"); // returns 4
// tasks is now:
// ["Pay phone bill",
//   "Write best-selling novel",
//   "Walk the dog",
//   "Feed the cat"]
```

reverse

reverse will reverse the order of the items in the array:

```
var tasks = [
  "Pay phone bill",
  "Write best-selling novel",
  "Walk the dog"
];

tasks.reverse();
// tasks is now:
// ["Walk the dog",
//   "Write best-selling novel",
//   "Pay phone bill"]
```

shift

shift removes the first item in the array and returns it:

```
var tasks = [
  "Pay phone bill",
  "Write best-selling novel",
  "Walk the dog"
];

tasks.shift(); // returns "Pay phone bill"
// tasks is now:
// ["Write best-selling novel",
//   "Walk the dog"]
```

sort

As the name implies, sort sorts the items of an array in ascending order. The sort algorithm is very basic. For example, regardless of whether you're sorting strings or numbers, everything is converted into strings and then compared. So if you're sorting [3, 10, 1, 2], rather than [1, 2, 3, 10], you'll end up with [1, 10, 2, 3]. That's because lexically (or alphabetically), 10 comes before 2 because it starts with a 1.

Thankfully, sort lets you pass in a custom comparison function:

```
array.sort([compare]);
```

This allows you to compare the items being sorted using your own criteria, without converting to strings if you don't want to. You can write a compare function to simply reverse the sort order, or to sort according to a highly customized set of criteria; for example, the second-last letter of the second-last word of each item in the array, if you so desired.

We'll take a closer look at the compare function a little later in the book once we've tackled functions. For now, here's how a simple sort works:

```
var tasks = [
  "Pay phone bill",
  "Write best-selling novel",
  "Walk the dog"
];

tasks.sort(); // sorts array in ascending order
// tasks is now:
// ["Pay phone bill",
//    "Walk the dog",
//    "Write best-selling novel"]
```

splice

```
array.splice(index, howMany[, element1, ...[, elementN]]);
```

splice lets you perform selective surgery on an array, allowing you to simultaneously add and remove items from an array with just one command:

splice.html (excerpt)

```
var tasks = [
  "Pay phone bill",
  "Write best-selling novel",
  "Walk the dog"
];

tasks.splice(1, 1, "World domination");
// tasks is now:
// ["Pay phone bill",
//    "World domination",
//    "Walk the dog"]
```

We just told `splice` to start at the index of 1, which was the position of `"Write best-selling novel"`, remove one item (removing `"Write best-selling novel"`), and then insert the item `"World domination"` in that position. We could do the same with multiple items:

```
var tasks = [
  "Pay phone bill",
  "Write best-selling novel",
  "Walk the dog"
];

tasks.splice(1, 1, "World domination", "Rotate tires",
"Hire hit squad");
  // tasks is now:
  // ["Pay phone bill",
  // "World domination",
  // "Rotate tires",
  // "Hire hit squad",
  // "Walk the dog"]
```

There are two points to note here. We've now have three items where `"Write best-selling novel"` used to be, and the inserted items have shifted `"Walk the dog"` without overwriting it.

Of course, there's no need to add any items when splicing. We could just remove items (and have them returned to us):

```
var tasks, task;

tasks = [
  "Pay phone bill",
  "Write best-selling novel",
  "Walk the dog"
];
task = tasks.splice(1, 1);
// returns "Write best-selling novel
alert("REMINDER! Don't forget to: " + task);
```

Here, all we're doing is slicing out `"Write best-selling novel"` and storing it in the variable named `task`. We then trigger an `alert` with the message: `"REMINDER! Don't forget to: Write best-selling novel"`. This can be seen in Figure 3.2.

Figure 3.2. Alert showing a reminder message

 Getting the User's Attention

An **alert** is a basic way to attract the user's attention. It's hardly an elegant way of doing it, but it's simple and achieves the task required—especially for the purposes of this book!

Unfortunately, users are unable to interact with the page while an **alert** message is active. They first need to click the **"OK"** button in order to dismiss the message first.

unshift

unshift adds one or more items to the beginning of the array and returns the array's new length:

unshift.html (excerpt)

```
var tasks, len;

tasks = [
  "Pay phone bill",
  "Write best-selling novel",
  "Walk the dog"
];
len = tasks.unshift("Defeat nemesis", "Pick up dry
```

```
➡cleaning");
        alert("You now have " + len + " tasks to complete: "
➡+ tasks.join(", "));
```

Here, we've simply added two new tasks to the beginning of our list using `unshift`, then taken the array's new length and constructed a message for the user. The result is shown in Figure 3.3.

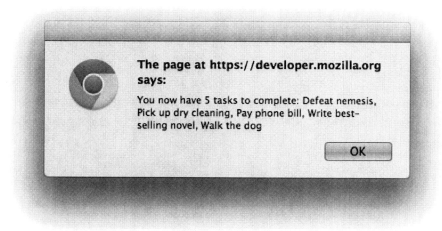

Figure 3.3. Alert showing new number of tasks

You may have noticed my use of the `join` method. We'll take a look at `join` shortly.

Accessor Methods

concat

With `concat`, you can combine two or more arrays into one. The original arrays being concatenated remain untouched. The operation returns a newly formed array with the concatenated values in it:

```
var arr1, arr2, arr3, arr4;

arr1 = ["Pay phone bill"];
arr2 = ["Write best-selling novel"];
arr3 = ["Walk the dog"];
arr4 = arr1.concat(arr2, arr3);
```

```
// arr4 contains:
// ["Pay phone bill",
//    "Write best-selling novel",
//    "walk the dog"]
```

Here, the `concat` method has filled `arr4` with the contents of the first three arrays. The other three arrays remain unchanged, each still containing one item.

join

We've already seen `join` in action in the `unshift` example. `join` takes the values in an array and joins them into a string. You can pass it a parameter to specify what character(s) to put in between each item as it performs the join operation. If you don't, it will just output a comma-separated list of items. Note that it doesn't matter what type each of the array items are—`join` will perform a `toString` conversion on each item and use the result (we'll look at `toString` in just a moment), as shown in Figure 3.4:

```
                                                              join.html
var nums;

nums = [4, 8, 15, 16, 23, 42];
alert("The winning lottery numbers are: "
➥+ nums.join(", "));
```

Figure 3.4. Alert showing `join` in action

You may be asking why a comma was passed in for that example when calling `join` by itself would have automatically inserted a comma. Notice how there's a space after the comma? Otherwise, we'd end up with `The winning lottery numbers are: 4,8,15,16,23,42`, as shown in Figure 3.5.

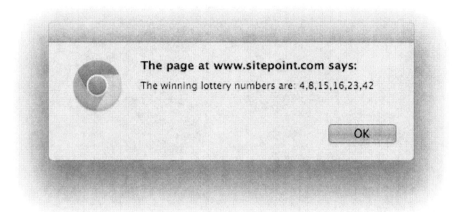

Figure 3.5. Alert showing `join` in action without spacing

slice

`slice` will copy a part of an array and return it. Rather than modify the original array, it just makes a shallow copy. You tell it where to start and, optionally, where to end copying. So `arr.slice(2)` will return a copy of `arr` starting at index 2 and going all the way to the end of the array. Conversely, `arr.slice(-2)` will start at the end and give you the last two items. `arr.slice(2, 4)` will make a copy of `arr` from index 2 to index 4.

Did you see we said that `slice` makes a *shallow* copy? For example, if your array contains an array as one of its items, it will be copied by reference. In other words, if the original array changes, so will the copy.

Let's create a task list that has a child list of cleaning-related items, then copy it and slice it up into smaller lists:

```
         var tasks, todo, cleanup, noCleaning;

         tasks = [
                 "Fly a kite",
                 "Save the world",
                 [
                   "Clean bathroom",
                   "Clean garage",
                   "Clean up act"
                 ]
               ];
         todo = tasks.slice(0); // makes a copy of tasks
         cleanup = tasks.slice(-1); // copies only the nested array
         noCleaning = tasks.slice(0, 2);
➥// copies only the first two items
```

The first point to note is that the third item in the `tasks` list is an array. We've already mentioned that `slice` makes a shallow copy of the array. This is an example of needing to be careful when making a sliced copy, because the child array will only be copied by reference. In other words, the copy of the child array will be pointing to the original, so if the original array changes, the copy will change too.

toString

`toString` returns a string representing the array and its items:

```
         var arr = ["These", "words", "are",
➥ "separated", "by", "commas"];

         arr.toString(); //
➥returns "These,words,are,separated,by,commas"
```

When array items are exclusively strings, as in the previous example, they're simply concatenated in a comma-separated list and returned. Numbers are first converted to strings before the concatenation:

```
         var arr = ["These", 8, "words", "and", "numbers", "are",
➥ "separated", "by", "commas"];

         arr.toString(); // returns
➥"These,8,words,and,numbers,are,separated,by,commas"
```

In the case of arrays and objects (which we'll cover later), we see a different behavior:

```
        var arr = ["a", "b", "c", 100, 200, 300, [1,2,3],
➥{"foo": "bar"}];

        arr.toString(); // returns "a,b,c,100,200,300,1,2,3,
➥[object Object]"
```

Note how the toString function flattens out the nested array containing the values 1,2,3, but only outputs [object Object] for the object literal.

indexOf

indexOf will find the first instance of an item in an array and return its index to you. It does this using strict equality, just like when you use === instead of ==. Here's an example:

```
        array.indexOf(searchElement, [fromIndex]);
```

The searchElement value is what you're looking for. If you know that your value occurs after a certain point, you can optionally pass an index from which to begin the search so that you can avoid looking through the whole array, as shown in Figure 3.6:

```
        var alphabet;

        alphabet = ["a", "b", "c", "d", "e", "f", "g", "h", "i",
➥ "j", "k", "l", "m", "n", "o", "p", "q", "r", "s", "t", "u", "v",
➥ "w", "x", "y", "z"];
        alert("The letter 'm' is at index: " +
➥alphabet.indexOf("m"));
```

Figure 3.6. Alert showing result of `indexOf` search

You might pass in an index at which to start the search, like `alphabet.indexOf("m", 10)`. In this case, there will be little difference as the number of items in the array is so small. But in very large arrays, it could have an impact on performance because you'll have much fewer items to search through.

lastIndexOf

`lastIndexOf` works exactly like `indexOf`, but begins its search from the end of the array rather than the beginning. Thus, it will find the last occurrence of the `searchElement`:

```
array.lastIndexOf(searchElement, [fromIndex]);
```

Iteration Methods

forEach (JavaScript 1.6)

Traditionally, when you wanted to work with all the items in an array, you'd loop over it. Though we'll be covering loops later, it's important to show you how it used to be done so that you understand why the `forEach` method is handy.

The following is a program that uses the traditional method of looping over an array. The array contains a set of numbers, and on each pass, the instructions in the loop add the current number to the total. The program ends with an alert stating the total amount, which is 108:

forach.html (excerpt)

```
var arr, i, num, total;

arr = [4, 8, 15, 16, 23, 42];
total = 0;

for (i = 0; i < arr.length; i = i + 1) {
  num = arr[i];
  total = total + num;
}

alert("The total is: " + total);
```

Figure 3.7 shows how that looks.

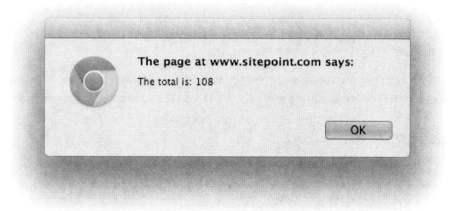

Figure 3.7. An alert showing the total value of the numbers in an array

Though there are several ways to create a loop, the `for` loop seen in this example is the most common. It consists of three parts: the initialization (`i = 0`), the condition (`i < arr.length`), and the final expression (`i = i + 1`). The loop starts with the variable `i` set to zero. If the value of `i` is less than the length of the array, which it is, the loop's body is executed once. After the body is executed, `i` is incremented by one. This process continues until `i` is no longer less than `arr.length`. Now that you have a basic understanding of the `for` loop, take a look at how `forEach` can simplify the same program:

```
var arr, total;

arr = [4, 8, 15, 16, 23, 42];
total = 0;

arr.forEach(function(num) {
  total = total + num;
});

alert("The total is: " + total);
```

Notice how the loop itself is now a call to the array's `forEach` method. We pass in an anonymous function (we'll cover those in detail later) that receives a value as an argument and places it in the variable `num`. In other words, each time `forEach` steps over a number in the array, it passes it to this function as `num`. The rest is just math, and the total displayed in the `alert` ends up being identical, just as it did in the previous example.

map (JavaScript 1.6)

The `map` method is nearly identical to `forEach`. The only difference is that `map` returns an array containing the values returned by the callback function. The following example uses `map` to compute the square of each item in `arr`. The results are then returned and stored in `squared`:

map.html (excerpt)

```
var arr = [1, 2, 3, 4, 5];
var squared;

squared = arr.map(function(num) {
  return (num * num);
}); // squared is [1, 4, 9, 16, 25]
```

every (JavaScript 1.6)

Sometimes, you need to validate that the data in an array conforms to a set of criteria. You could, as in the previous example, run a manual test using either a traditional `for` loop or the `forEach` method. Or you could just use the `every` method that runs a callback function against each item in the array. It will return `true` if they all conform, or `false` if one or more fails to:

```
                                                        every.html (excerpt)

var arr, isValid;

arr = [1, 2, 3, 4, 5];
isValid = arr.every(function(num) {
  return (num < 10);
}); // isValid is true
```

In this example, we're using the `every` method to check that every item in our array is less than 10. The `every` method loops over the array, and for each item it runs the function we've included within its parentheses. The current array item is passed in as `num`, and our expression (`return (num < 10)`) checks to see if the number is less than 10, returning `true` or `false`. `every` monitors the response from our code and if we ever return `false`, it kicks out of the loop and returns `false`. We capture its response in the variable `isValid`. In the case above, the `every` method will return `true`. If we change our expression to check if numbers are greater than 3, then `isValid` will be `false`:

```
var arr, isValid;

arr = [1, 2, 3, 4, 5];
isValid = arr.every(function(num) {
  return (num < 3);
}); // isValid is false
```

some (JavaScript 1.6)

You can use `some` to check if one or more of the items in an array conform to a test. `some` works just like `every`, but will return `true` as long as one array item returns `true`:

```
                                                        some.html (excerpt)

var arr, isValid;

arr = [1, 2, 3, 4, 5];
```

```
isValid = arr.some(function(num) {
  return (num < 2);
}); // isValid is true
```

In this example, even though just the one number in the array is less than 2, `isValid` is still `true`.

filter (JavaScript 1.6)

It's all well and good to test an array, but what if you want to create a new array with the items that met your criteria? Well, `filter` does just that. It works like `every` and `some` do, except that any item that passes your criteria is copied into a new array:

filter.html (excerpt)

```
var arr, filtered;

arr = [1, 2, 3, 4, 5, 6, 7, 8, 9];
filtered = arr.filter(function(num) {
  return (num < 5);
});
// filtered now contains [1, 2, 3, 4]
```

reduce and reduceRight (JavaScript 1.8)

At times it's necessary to perform a mathematical operation on the array and reduce it to a single value; for instance, if you want the sum of the values in an array. This is where `reduce` (and `reduceRight`) come into play. `reduce` loops over an array and passes in a `previous` and `current` value. It also passes in the current index and a reference to the array itself, should you need them in your calculations. For this example, however, we'll be using the `previous` and `current` arguments only:

reduce.html (excerpt)

```
var arr, total;

arr = [1, 2, 3, 4, 5];
total = arr.reduce(function(previous, current) {
  return previous + current;
}); // total is 15
```

Here, `reduce` is running over the array just as the earlier methods did, but with a couple of big differences. For one, on the first pass, since there's no a `previous` value to pass in, the first and second items of the array are passed in (the values 1 and 2 in this case). On subsequent passes, the `previous` value is what your code returns, and the `current` value is the next item in the array. What we're doing here is taking the current item in the array and adding it to the previous value: the running total. The end result is that we add all the array's values together for the total value of 15.

`reduceRight` performs the same function as `reduce` but in reverse. In other words, it starts at the end of the array and moves towards the start.

Project

Our intention is to build a fully functional task manager (or a to-do app, if you like), but since we've only covered variables and arrays up to this point, we've been unable to write that much code yet. In the previous chapter, we created three separate variables holding three distinct tasks. Let's now put those three tasks in an array called `tasks`:

project.js

```
var tasks;

tasks = [
        "Pay phone bill",
        "Write best-selling novel",
        "Walk the dog"
      ];
```

Summary

This chapter has introduced arrays, and a number of methods for working with them. However, in JavaScript, arrays are actually objects, so to truly understand arrays you need to understand objects as well. Don't worry, though; objects are covered in detail in the next chapter.

Objects and Functions

In the previous chapter, we looked at arrays. Now we're going to look at objects, which are similar to arrays in that they are containers for collections of data. Though there are similarities—arrays are actually a type of object—there are also some significant differences.

Objects

Creating an Object

As with arrays, there are a couple of ways to create objects, and, just like arrays, one is preferred over the other. So even though you can do this:

```
var myObject = new Object();
```

it is much better to do this:

```
var myObject = {};
```

The latter is simpler, safer, and therefore preferable. If you remember from Chapter 3, `Array()` can be overwritten for malicious purposes. So can `Object()`, which is why it's safer to use the object literal notation `{}` as it's unable to be overwritten. The object literal represents a new, empty object.

Whereas in an array, values are simply added and accessed by index, objects use a key/value pair system. These two distinct ways of storing values make it fairly simple when choosing between arrays or objects for your data storage and retrieval needs. For example:

```
var lotteryNumbers, profile;

lotteryNumbers = [4, 8, 15, 16, 23, 42];
profile = {
  firstName: "Hugo",
  lastName: "Reyes",
  flight: "Oceanic 815",
  car: "Camaro"
};
```

Note how the `lotteryNumbers` array lends itself well to storing the sequence of lottery numbers, while the `profile` object is perfect for storing the key/value pairs of a person's (Hugo's) profile.

Adding to an Object

As you may have already noticed in the previous section, you can declare either an empty object, `{}`, or one with values in it (Hugo's profile). After you've declared your object, however, you can still add key/value pairs to it in a couple of ways. When looking at the chapter on arrays, we touched on named indices, which can be used to create associative arrays, though objects are better suited to the task. Here's an example of that:

```
var obj = {};

obj["firstName"] = "Hugo";
obj["lastName"] = "Reyes";
```

This is known as bracket notation. The alternative and more common syntax is dot notation. Here's an example:

```
var obj = {};

obj.firstName = "Hugo";
obj.lastName = "Reyes";
```

Dot notation is simpler than bracket notation; however, there are certain tasks that can only be done with bracket notation. For example, you can use a variable inside the brackets, which can't be done using dot notation. Bracket notation also supports strings containing spaces and other characters that are invalid in dot notation.

Reading from an Object

Reading a value from an object can also be accomplished using bracket or dot notation:

```
var obj = {};

obj.firstName = "Hugo";
obj.lastName = "Reyes";
alert("Hello, my name is " + obj.firstName + " "
➥+ obj.lastName + ".");
```

The result of running this code is shown in Figure 4.1.

Figure 4.1. Alert showing message coming from an object

Unlike arrays, it's not possible to read the contents of an object using a numeric index. The only type of index that can be used is a named one:

```
var obj = {};

obj.firstName = "Hugo";

obj[0];              // returns undefined
obj["firstName"]; // returns "Hugo"
obj.firstName;      // returns "Hugo"
```

Nested Objects

Nesting objects can be very helpful in organizing your data:

```
var person;

person = {
  name: {
    first: "Hugo",
    last: "Reyes"
  }
};
person.name.first; // returns "Hugo"
person.name.last;  // returns "Reyes"
```

It's also possible to assign objects:

```
var person;

person = {};
person.name = {};
person.name.first = "Hugo";
person.name.last = "Reyes";
```

Note, however, that the following will fail to work:

```
var person;

person = {};
person.name.first = "Hugo";
```

This will throw the error `TypeError: Cannot set property 'first' of undefined`, which means that it's trying to create `first` off `name`, which was never defined. In the prior example, we assigned an object to `person.name`, but not in this one.

Namespacing through Nested Objects

If you're at all familiar with modern programming languages, you've heard of **namespacing**. Essentially, it's a better way to organize code by putting it into nested buckets, or namespaces:

```
        Project.Strings.Warnings.sessionExpired =
➡ "Your session has expired."
```

Of course, in order for this namespace to exist, we must first nest the appropriate objects:

```
var Project = {
   Strings: {
     Warnings: {}
   }
};
```

Though this code sets up the required namespace, what happens if one or all of the objects in question are already there? And what if they already contain data?

Say, for example, we had the following:

```
var Project = {
   Strings: {
     Warnings: {
       overQuota: "You've exceeded your quota!",
       outOfStock: "We're out of stock!"
     }
   }
};
```

Now say elsewhere in our program (in a different JavaScript file) we wanted to add `Widgets` to the `Project` namespace, but were unsure whether it was already defined:

```
var Project = {
    Widgets: {}
};
```

By doing what we just did, we've destroyed the existing `Strings` object because we've overwritten the whole `Project` object with a new one. What we should be doing instead is checking to see if a `Project` object already exists. If so, we add to it; otherwise, we create it and then add to it:

```
var Project = Project || {};

Project.Widgets = {};
```

Here we use the OR operator (| |) to test whether or not `Project` is defined. If `Project` is already defined, it assigns its value to `Project` and nothing is changed. If it isn't, JavaScript assigns what's on the right-hand side of | | to the `Project` variable, which is shown in Figure 4.2

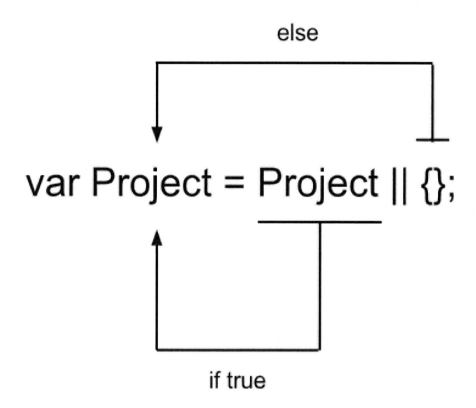

Figure 4.2. Demonstration of || operator in action

Prototype Chain

We're going to discuss looping over objects shortly, but in order to do that, we need to first cover JavaScript's prototype chain. You'll see why in just a second. For the time being, let's take a quick look at prototypes, because we'll be covering them in more detail later in the section on functions. For now, it's important to understand a little bit about them and how they affect looping over key/values in objects.

All objects have a prototype. So, what's a **prototype**? It's an object from which other objects inherit properties. Figure 4.3 presents a diagram illustrating the concept of prototypal inheritance.

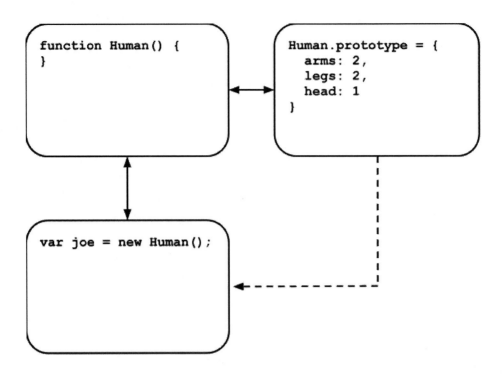

Figure 4.3. The prototype chain

As you can see, the Human prototype has arms, legs, and head properties that joe inherits when he's instantiated from Human. We'll look at object instantiation when we cover functions; for now, it's enough to know that joe gets his arms, legs, and head from Human.

Looping over an Object

Looping over an object isn't as simple as looping over an array. With an array, you simply increment an index value and use that to step through the array. With objects, there is no index value. Objects are collections of key/value pairs, so you need to step through them differently:

```
var data, key;

data = {
  firstName: "James",
```

```
    lastName: "Kirk",
    occupation: "Captain"
};

for (key in data) {
  alert(key + " is " + data[key]);
}
```

In this example, we use a `for ... in` loop. We give it a variable (in this case, `key`) that will be used to hold the key as it steps through the object, and an object to step over (in this case, `data`). For each key/value pair inside `data`, the loop will assign the key to our variable named `key`. Inside the body of the loop, we can use the key to plug into our object to access its associated value: `data[key]`. That's the equivalent of writing `data["firstName"]`, and on a subsequent pass, `data["lastName"]`, and so on.

There is one catch, though. Since objects inherit from objects, the loop may start returning key/value pairs from further up the prototype chain. To prevent this, we need to add something to our loop:

```
var data, key;

data = {
  firstName: "James",
  lastName: "Kirk",
  occupation: "Captain"
};

for (key in data) {
  if (data.hasOwnProperty(key)) {
    alert(key + " is " + data[key]);
  }
}
```

The `hasOwnProperty` method makes sure that the key we're using belongs to the object in question and doesn't originate further up the prototype chain. If it returns `true`, we can proceed with our operation. Otherwise, we ignore it.

Functions

As you write more complex programs, you'll find the need to achieve certain operations that JavaScript doesn't do natively. You can accomplish the job with just a few lines of code, but it's likely you'll want to perform that job more than once. That's where functions come in. A **function** is a way to group a set of operations, give it a name, and then be able to call it as often as you wish. Here's a simple function:

```
function sayHello() {
   alert("Hello, world!");
}
```

By calling this simple function, you can cause an alert to appear with the message, "Hello, world!". Once we've defined sayHello (as we did above), running (or executing or calling) it is very simple; you just write its name followed by parentheses:

```
sayHello();
```

The reason for the parentheses is so that you can pass values as arguments into your function. For example, rather than our function saying "Hello, world!", we could have it say something else:

```
function sayHello(msg) {
   alert(msg);
}
```

Now when we call sayHello, we can pass in our own message:

```
sayHello("Howdy, y'all!");
```

Doing this calls the sayHello function and passes in "Howdy, y'all!" as the first argument. If you look at our sayHello function, we've specified a variable named msg as the first argument, so inside sayHello, msg will contain the value that was passed into the function; in this case, "Howdy, y'all!" We then hand that variable over to alert and voilà!

Before we go any further with functions, we need to cover the important topics of scope and hoisting. These can occur as a result of using functions, and if you're unaware of them, you may run into trouble—such as code behaving strangely.

Scope

Not only are functions containers for groups of operations, they also create a scope for variables. Variables exist either in the **global scope** (not declared within a function and available everywhere) or **local scope** (declared within a function and only available within it). No code outside the function can access a variable declared within it. Only code inside the function can access it. Nested function declarations that are declared at the same level or lower than the variable can also access it. So, for example:

```
function hi() {
  var hello = "hello"
};

hi();
alert(hello);
```

In this case, the variable named `hello` is scoped to the `hi` function. This means that the `alert` trying to access the `hello` variable from outside the `hi` function will be unable to. Instead, it will receive a `ReferenceError: hello is not defined` error. The reason why is because the variable `hello` was declared inside of `hi` and is therefore scoped to `hi`. It's unavailable outside of the `hi` function.

That said, any function declared within another function automatically has access to variables declared within its parent function:

scope-1.html (excerpt)

```
function fullName() {
  var firstName = "Hugo";

  function alertFullName() {
    var lastName = "Reyes";

    alert("Full name: " + firstName + " " + lastName);
  }
```

```
        alertFullName();
    }

    fullName();
```

Figure 4.4 shows what that looks like.

Figure 4.4. Concatenation of scoped variable values

The outer function, fullName, creates a scope inside which the variable firstName and function alertFullName are declared. Since they're both declared inside fullName's scope, alertFullName has access to firstName. So when fullName is executed, and it in turn executes alertFullName, alertFullName is able to access both its own lastName variable as well as its parent's firstName to put together its alert text, as shown in Figure 4.5.

Figure 4.5. Variable scoping illustrated

In fact, a function has access to all variables declared above it, no matter how deeply it's nested. Let's illustrate this. For this example, we'll use the console's `log` function to output values directly to the browser's console. If you're yet to use the console, go back to the first chapter and quickly review how to enable your browser's console for this next example:

scope-2.html (excerpt)

```
// Declaring a global variable and giving it the value "a"
var a = "a";

function levelb() {
  // Declaring a variable that levelb and children can see
  var b = "b";

  function levelc() {
```

```
            // Declaring a variable only levelc and leveld can see
            var c = "c";

            function leveld() {
                // Declaring a variable only leveld can see
                var d = "d";

                console.log("leveld", a, b, c, d);
            }

            // Running leveld() will output a, b, c and d
            leveld();

            console.log("levelc", a, b, c);
        }

        // Running levelc() will output a, b, and c
        levelc();

        console.log("levelb", a, b);
    }

    // Running levelb() will output a and b
    levelb();

    // Only the variable named "a" is available globally
    console.log("global", a);
```

If you run this example, you'll end up with the following output in your browser's console:

```
leveld a b c d
levelc a b c
levelb a b
global a
```

As you can see in Figure 4.6, nested function declarations can access variables declared above them. To avoid confusion, here we only drew arrows from the var a declaration to show how it becomes available to the child function declarations.

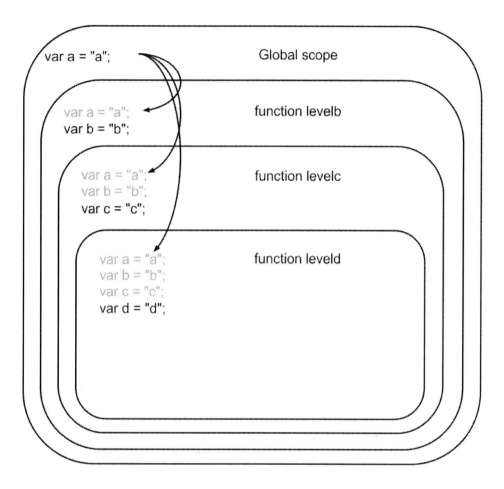

Figure 4.6. An example of variable scoping

Hoisting

Now that we've covered how functions create variable scope, we'll address a phenomenon called hoisting. Because JavaScript is a very permissive language, it has
to do a lot of work under the hood. We've already seen this with type coercion,
when JavaScript attempts to convert variable types in order to make operations with
conflicting types work. **Hoisting** is another "under the hood" action by JavaScript
where it moves all variable declarations to the top of a function. That means that
this:

```
    var name = "Emma";

    function nameHer() {
      var name;
      console.log(name); // outputs undefined
      name = "Audrey";
    }
```

is the same as:

```
    var name = "Emma";

    function nameHer() {
      console.log(name); // outputs undefined
      name = "Audrey";
      var name;
    }
```

which is the same as:

```
    var name = "Emma";

    function nameHer() {
      console.log(name); // outputs undefined
      var name = "Audrey";
    }
```

All three examples are the same because JavaScript reads the body of those functions, and moves all the variable declarations to the top of the function. Note that it only moves the declaration, not the assignment. Under the hood, all three functions end up looking like the first. That's why the second and third examples output undefined rather that "Emma" as you'd expect. Even though it looks as though we're using the name variable containing "Emma" before assigning "Audrey" to it, we're actually declaring a new and undefined name variable at the top of each function.

Declaration

So far, we've seen one of three possible ways to create a function. Not only can we use the function statement (or declaration), we can also use the function operator (or expression) and the Function constructor. The first is a named function declaration, the second is a function expression, and the third is a constructor just like

`Array()` and `Object()`. As with `Array()` and `Object()`, the `Function()` constructor returns a new `Function` object:

```
// declaration
function sayHello1() {
  alert("Hello");
}

// expression
var sayHello2 = function() {
  alert("Hello");
};

// constructor (not recommended)
var sayHello3 = new Function("alert('Hello')");
```

Let's start by taking a look at the first two, since they're the most common. They have a couple of differences between them, the first being that a function declaration needs to have a name (in this case, `sayHello1`). If the function declaration has no name, it's considered a function expression and, since it's nameless, an anonymous function. Why does this matter? Well, the second distinction between function declarations and expressions is the way in which the JavaScript engine parses them. Function declarations are hoisted just as variables are, while only the variable declaration of a function expression is hoisted. For example, this is possible with a function declaration:

```
alert(hi());

function hi() {
  return "Hi!";
}
```

It's possible because the entire `hi` function is hoisted above `alert` and is therefore available when `alert` uses it. Now let's look at a similar example using a function expression, which will throw a `TypeError: undefined is not a function` error:

```
alert(hey());

var hey = function () {
  return "Hey!";
};
```

The reason the error says "undefined is not a function" is because at run time, the hey variable declaration is hoisted above the alert but the assignment of the function remains below.

The third way of writing a function is via the Function constructor. Of the three, it's the least recommended, as it requires your code to be passed in as a string, which is error-prone and difficult to write.

If you're going to use function declarations, always declare them at the top of your code's scope (be it the global or local scope) so as to avoid hoisting, and to make it clear to the reader when the function is actually available for use. If you're going to use function expressions, declare the variables you'll be assigning to your functions at the top of your local scope for the same reason. Whatever you do, avoid writing code where you conditionally declare functions because you'll run into inconsistent behavior across browsers, to say nothing of it being bad practice.

As of this writing, Google Chrome alerts "Hello!" while Mozilla Firefox alerts "Hi!" when running this code:

```
if (true) {
  function hello() {
    alert("Hi!");
  }
} else {
  function hello() {
    alert("Hello!");
  }
}
```

However, when written as function expressions, both browsers will return "Hi!" because only the true branch of the if statement will ever be executed and therefore parsed:

```
var hello;

if (true) {
  hello = function() {
    alert("Hi!");
  }
} else {
  hello = function() {
```

```
        alert("Hello!");
    }
}
```

Arguments

When you define a function, you can define a list of arguments that it will receive. In doing so, you're declaring variables for use within the scope of that function. In other words, those variables can only be used inside that function. For example:

function-arguments.html (excerpt)

```
function person(firstName, lastName, age) {
  alert(firstName);
  alert(lastName);
  alert(age);
}

person("John", "Doe", 44);
```

Our function, named `person`, receives three arguments, `firstName`, `lastName`, and `age`. When the function is called on the last line of our example, three values are passed through its parentheses: `"John"`, `"Doe"`, and `44`. Inside the function, we take those three values and `alert` them one after the other.

Sometimes, however, it's not possible or ideal to predefine arguments. If we wanted to create a function that concatenated an arbitrary number of values and returned the result, how would we define the argument list? Well, JavaScript functions have a special array-like object called `arguments` that we can access from within the function to see exactly what was passed in:

arguments-variable.html

```
function concatenate() {
  var i, str;

  str = "";
  for (i = 0; i < arguments.length; i += 1) {
    str += arguments[i];
  }
  return str;
}
```

```
        concatenate("Super", "cali", "fragilistic", "expiali",
➥ "docious");
        // returns Supercalifragilisticexpialidocious
```

We have no way of knowing how many strings will be passed into our `concatenate` function, so we're unable to predefine a list of arguments. Instead, we loop over the special `arguments` array and concatenate the values from there.

Of course, this is a simple example of a function in action, and a useless one at that, since we could just call `alert` on our own without wrapping it in a function. But say we wanted to take a string and translate it into Pig Latin? We could write a function that receives a value and then returns another. In order to get something back, we need to make use of the `return` statement:

pig-latin.html (excerpt)

```
function pigLatin(phrase) {
  var words, pigged;

  // Create an array with the words of the phrase
  //   we're given by splitting the phrase on the
  //   spaces between the words.
  words = phrase.split(" ");

  // Loop over the words array and translate each word to
  //   Pig Latin. Return the translated word so that it
  //   gets placed in a new array called "pigged."
  pigged = words.map(function (word) {
    var first, rest;

    // Grab the first letter of the word
    first = word.substring(0, 1);

    // Grab the rest of the word
    rest = word.substring(1);

    // Start the new word with the ending of the old word,
    //   and add the first letter of the old word as well as
    //   "ay" to the end of it. Return the result of the
    //   concatenation so that the map function can add it
    //   to the "pigged" array.
    return rest + first + "ay";
```

```
    });

    // Rebuild the new Pig Latin phrase by rejoining the newly
    //   "pigged" words with spaces in between. Return the
    //   result so that anyone calling our pigLatin function
    //   can actually get the new Pig Latin version of their
    //   phrase.
    return pigged.join(" ");
}
```

Then, we could pass it a simple phrase and have the Pig Latin version returned to us:

```
var pl = pigLatin("tonight you belong to me");

// returns "onighttay ouyay elongbay otay emay" into pl
```

Now, whenever we want to translate a phrase, we just need to pass it into our pigLatin function and we have our translation. Simple!

Object-oriented Programming with Functions

Unfortunately, providing an in-depth, comprehensive explanation of what **object-oriented programming (OOP)** is falls outside the scope of this short book. But the basic gist of it is that OOP is a programming style that lets you represent real-world items as objects in your code. An object can represent a physical element such as a person or fruit, or something more abstract such as a bank account or network connection. The object stores data (called properties) and functions (called methods), the latter acting on the data. So an object representing a bank account may have properties such as account number, balance, and overdraft limit, and methods such as deposit and withdraw.

For anyone familiar with traditional class-based OOP, JavaScript is a class-less prototypal programming language where objects inherit from other objects instead of classes. JavaScript uses functions as classes but has no **class** statement. Instead, any function can act as a class and new instances of that class can be created using the new keyword:

```
var checking, savings;

// This is the definition of our Account class
function Account(accountNumber) {
  // This is the property we'll be storing the
  //   account number in.
  this.accountNumber = accountNumber;

  // This is the property we'll be tracking the
  //   account's funds in.
  this.funds = 0;

  // This is the setter method we'll be using to
  //   add funds to the account.
  this.deposit = function(amount) {
    if (amount === Number(amount)) {
      this.funds += amount;
    }
  };

  // This is the getter method that returns the
  //   account's balance.
  this.balance = function() {
    return this.funds;
  };
}

// The "new Account()" constructor returns a new account
//   object complete with deposit and balance methods. We
//   store the account object in a variable called checking.
checking = new Account("87654321");

// Using the deposit method allows us to pass values to
//   our account object.
checking.deposit(12.35);
checking.deposit(2.76);
checking.deposit(74.01);

// We now create a new account object and store that in a
//   variable called savings. It also has deposit and
//   balance methods, and is distinct from the "checking"
//   account object.
savings = new Account("12345678");
```

```
savings.deposit(225.57);

// Using the objects' balance method, we can ask each
//   of them to report their balances.
checking.balance(); // returns 89.12
savings.balance(); // returns 225.57
```

Here, we have a function called Account from which two instances are created, checking and savings. By using the this keyword inside the function and hanging variables and functions off it, we've effectively created a class function used for instantiation. Now we can create instances of this function using the new keyword, which we do to create both the checking and savings objects in our example. In this case, the this keyword refers to the account object that was instantiated so that the deposit and balance methods—as well as the funds property—belong exclusively to the object instance. This way, we can have multiple coexisting instances of each with their own properties and methods.

Note that although it's possible to directly read from and write to the funds property by typing checking.funds = 100 or alert(checking.funds), it's sometimes better to go through the getter and setter methods. In this case, we have a deposit method so as to ensure that the value passed in is actually a number. We have a balance method just to demonstrate how a getter would work. You can also access the checking.accountNumber property directly.

Because JavaScript lets you use regular functions as classes, developers have adopted a naming convention that makes functions intended to be used as classes easier to identify. A function that's intended to be used as a class has an uppercase first letter, while regular functions start with a lowercase first letter:

```
// this is intended to be used as a class
function Account() {
}

// this is not
function jump() {
}
```

`this`

The `this` keyword can be tricky to work with, as what it refers to depends entirely on how it's used. We saw one example of its use in the `Account` object example earlier. In that case, `this` referred to the object we instantiated. Depending on context, though, `this` points to different things, and it's important to know what it's referring to.

For example, in Figure 4.7 it refers to the global `window` object when used in a regular function, while in a constructor it refers to the function itself. In a regular function inside an object literal, the `this` keyword refers to the immediate parent object, while in an event handler, it refers to the DOM element that called the handler. And, of course, when using either the `call` or `apply` methods to execute a function, we can pass in an object for the `this` keyword to refer to. Let's go over each of those one by one.

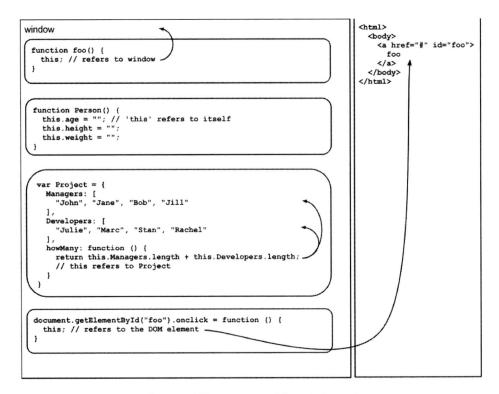

Figure 4.7. Different contexts of the `this` keyword

Simple Function

When the `this` keyword is used inside a simple function, it refers to the global variable scope, which is the `window` object. In this context, there's no real need to use the `this` keyword as any variable in the global scope is accessible simply by using its name. In other words, if you declare a variable named `foo` globally, you can just refer to it as `foo`; no need to use `this.foo`. JavaScript is simply referring you to the global scope because there's nothing else for it to point the `this` keyword to in this instance. If you're running in strict mode, however, it will return `undefined`. This is to prevent unintentional errors that are bound to happen in this context.

 Strict Mode

Strict mode is a recent addition to JavaScript. By opting into strict mode via the addition of `"use strict"`; at the top of a function, you force the JavaScript engine to change its behavior and essentially fix some potentially error-prone ways of handling code. In this case, it's what `this` refers to in a simple function.

In a Constructor

When used in a constructor or function intended to be instantiated via the `new` keyword, `this` refers to the object that's to be created. So if your constructor is a bank account:

```
var Account, savings;

Account = function(num) {
  this.accountNumber = num;
};

savings = new Account(12345678);
savings.accountNumber; // returns 12345678
```

In this case, the `this` keyword lets you attach the `accountNumber` property to the object that's to be instantiated. It's therefore possible to get that value by referring to `savings.accountNumber`.

Inside an Object Literal

If your function happens to be inside an object literal, and it's a simple function call as in our first example, the `this` keyword now refers to the immediate parent object surrounding your function. For example, the code in our diagram has two arrays inside the `Project` object called `Managers` and `Developers`. The `howMany` function adds their lengths by referring to `this.Managers` and `this.Developers` respectively. That means that the call to the `this` keyword points us to the `Project` object from which we can drop down to both `Managers` and `Developers`.

Inside an Event Handler

We'll look at event handlers in detail later, but basically, an **event handler** is a function that is called when an event is triggered, such as a `"click"` event when a link is clicked on. In an event handler, the `this` keyword refers to the element that triggered the event, which in this case is the anchor on the page.

call and apply

It's possible to invoke a function using the `call` and `apply` methods that are provided. We'll cover these in more detail shortly, but in both cases, the first argument of these methods is an object you can pass in for the `this` keyword to refer to.

bind

Finally, ECMAScript 5 introduced a method called `bind` that creates a new function and permanently binds it to the object you pass it. That object gets referred to when calling `this`. We'll also address this in more detail soon.

Properties

constructor

If you're handed an object that's an instance of a function, you may want to know what that original function was. What's more, you may wish to instantiate another object off that original function. With the `constructor` property, you can. It returns a reference to the original function in question, which allows you to create new instances with the original data:

```
        var foo, bar, baz;

        function Foo() {
          this.ident = "foo";
        }

        foo = new Foo();
        foo.ident; // returns "foo"

        bar = new Foo();
        bar.ident;  // returns "foo"
        bar.ident = "bar";
        bar.ident;  // now returns "bar"

        baz = new bar.constructor();
        baz.ident; // returns "foo"
```

First, we instantiate foo, which has an ident property value of "foo". Next, we instantiate bar, whose ident is also "foo" since it comes from the Foo class. However, we change its ident value to "bar". We then instantiate baz by using bar's constructor property. The property points us to the original Foo function, which gives our baz instance the same original ident value of "foo".

length

If you ever need to know how many arguments a function is expecting, you can check with the length property:

```
        function foo(bar, baz) {
        }

        foo.length; // returns 2
```

We get the value 2 returned when checking the length of foo because it's expecting bar and baz as arguments.

Methods

`apply`

Sometimes, you need to change what a function's `this` keyword points to. The `apply` method makes it easy by letting you pass an object in as its first parameter that the `this` keyword will point to:

```javascript
var person, lastName;

lastName = "Reyes";
person = function() {
  return this.lastName;
};

person(); // returns "Reyes"

person.apply({lastName: "Cooper"}); // returns "Cooper"
```

In this example, our function refers originally to the globally declared `lastName` since in this case, `this` refers to `window`. But when we use `apply`, we pass in an object that the `this` keyword now points to, and hanging off it is a new `lastName` value. Therefore, when we use `apply` the return value is no longer `"Reyes"` but `"Cooper"`.

When calling `apply`, you can also pass the function an array of arguments:

```javascript
var tax;

tax = function(price, provincial, federal) {
  return price * provincial * federal;
};

tax.apply(null, [100, 1.05, 1.095]); // returns 114.975
```

Here, we have a tax function that takes a price, multiplies it by the provincial and federal tax rates, and returns the value. Since we aren't trying to change where the `this` keyword is pointing, we don't bother passing in a value for the first argument. Instead, we skip it by passing in `null`. We then pass in an array containing values for the price, and the provincial and federal tax rates.

call

The call method is almost identical to apply except that instead of passing in an array of arguments, you only pass arguments, just as you would when calling the function itself (starting from the second argument):

```
var tax;

tax = function(price, provincial, federal) {
  return price * provincial * federal;
};

tax.call(null, 100, 1.05, 1.095); // returns 114.975
```

Note how the only difference between this implementation and the one for apply is how we pass the price, provincial, and federal values. With apply, they're passed in an array, while here they're passed in as individual arguments.

bind

With ECMAScript 5, it's now possible to call the bind method off a function and pass in an object that will be referred to as this. The bind method creates a new function with the object bound to it:

```
var hugo, person, names;

person = function () {
  return this.lastName;
};

hugo = person.bind({lastName: "Reyes"});
hugo(); // returns "Reyes"

names = {
  lastName: "Cooper",
  hugo: hugo,
  person: person
};
names.hugo(); // returns "Reyes"
names.person(); // returns "Cooper"
```

You'll note how the person function points to this.lastName and that before we bind it, lastName refers to a variable in the global window space (which is undefined).

So we go ahead and bind it to an object containing a `lastName` property with the value of `"Reyes"`. Now, when we call the newly created `hugo` function, `"Reyes"` is returned to us from the object that was bound to it.

Say if we were to place the original `person` function as well as the newly created `hugo` function inside an object containing a `lastName` property. We would see how `this` inside `person` dynamically points to the outer object, and therefore `this.lastName` now returns `"Cooper"` while the permanently bound `hugo` function continues to return `"Reyes"`.

toString

The `toString` method returns a string representing the code of a function. So, for example, if we wrote a simple function:

```
function foo() {
  return "foo";
}
```

and then called `toString` on it:

```
foo.toString();
```

we'd have a response such as this:

```
"function foo() {
    return "foo";
  }"
```

If, however, we called `toString` on a function that's a part of the JavaScript language:

```
document.getElementById.toString()
```

we'd receive a response that looked as follows:

```
"function getElementById() { [native code] }"
```

That's because the code responsible for `getElementById` is compiled, and cannot be output in human-readable form as JavaScript can.

Project

Now that we have functions and objects figured out, we can start doing some fancy stuff with our task manager project. Instead of a simple array of tasks, we can store richer information by using an array of objects. We can also write some functions to perform operations for us. Let's begin by wrapping each task in an object:

project-1.js

```
var tasks;

tasks = [
  {
    text: "Pay phone bill",
    complete: false,
    priority: 1
  },
  {
    text: "Write best-selling novel",
    complete: false,
    priority: 3
  },
  {
    text: "Walk the dog",
    complete: false,
    priority: 2
  }
];
```

Now we have a richer set of data; each task now has a `complete` flag associated with it, as well as a `priority`. Let's write a function to add tasks to our array:

```
var tasks, addTask;

tasks = [];

addTask = function(task) {
  tasks.push({
    text: task,
    complete: false,
    priority: 1
  });
};
```

Now we can call `addTask`, and pass it some text to store it, with a `complete` flag set to `false` in our `tasks` array.

Summary

In this chapter, we covered objects, including how to write to and read from objects, and how to nest objects to create namespacing for variables. We also looked at looping over objects to read data, and how we can filter the prototype chain out when looping over object properties. We then went on to functions, exploring the different ways we can create them, as well as how we can use functions to write object-oriented code. We examined various properties and methods of functions, and finished off by adding our knowledge to the task manager project we're building.

In the next chapter, we'll take a look at looping and jumping.

5

Loops and Jumps

This chapter introduces loop and jump statements. A **loop statement** is used when we want to repeat some programming statements until a specified condition is reached. A typical example would be to iterate through a list and perform an operation on each member of the list. A **jump statement** allows code to exit loops. One example is to loop through our to-do list and then break out of the loop upon reaching the first incomplete item. There are various types of jump statements, which we'll explain as we go along.

Loops are generally associated with a particular style of programming known as **imperative programming**. Here, the programmer specifies step by step how a program should achieve a particular task. An alternative approach is **functional programming**, which states what the program should be doing without exactly specifying how the program should do it. JavaScript supports multiple paradigms including imperative and functional styles. We will spend the latter part of this chapter looking at some functional alternatives to working with loops. Functional programming can provide more elegant solutions to certain types of problems, and it can make your code base smaller, more understandable, and easier to maintain.

Loops

By way of introduction, we should note that as with the `if` statement, all looping constructs can be written without the enclosing curly braces when only a single statement is involved. For clarity, we recommend that you always include the curly braces, even for single statements. This is the standard that was followed by the team at id Software when they programmed Doom 3.[1] We say only partially tongue-in-cheek that if it's good enough for the legendary John Carmack and his team, it's certainly good enough for us!

The `while` Loop

The while loop takes the following form:

```
while (condition) {
    statement
}
```

The condition can be any expression that evaluates to `true` or `false`. The `statement` consists of the code that is executed while the condition evaluates to `true`. Recall that in JavaScript, any value can be converted to a Boolean. For those who need a refresher on how particular values in JavaScript are converted to Booleans, we refer you to this excellent article written by our technical editor, Colin Ihrig.[2]

The `while` loop can be illustrated with this simple example:

```
var tasksToDo = 3;

while (tasksToDo > 0) {
    console.log('There are ' + tasksToDo + ' tasks to do');
    tasksToDo--;
}
```

This prints the following to the console:

---

[1] https://github.com/id-Software/DOOM-3-BFG
[2] http://cjihrig.com/blog/truthy-and-falsy-in-javascript/

```
There are 3 tasks to do
There are 2 tasks to do
There are 1 tasks to do
```

When using a `while` loop, it's important to make sure that the condition eventually evaluates to `false`. During each iteration of the loop, some variable should be changing that will eventually lead to the condition being `false`, thereby terminating the loop. Otherwise, your program becomes stuck in the dreaded infinite loop. For an example of a subtle bug that leads to an infinite loop, consider this:

```
function getNext(num) {
    return num++;
}

var i=0;

while (i < 3) {
    i = getNext(i);
}
```

At first it may be hard to even spot the bug. Note that `num++` will return the value of `num`, and then increment the value. Therefore, in the `while` loop, the value of `i` will always be zero! Whenever you are writing a `while` loop, always double-check that the loop will gracefully exit. With patience and practice this will soon become second nature.

The `do ... while` Loop

The `do ... while` loop is a variation of the `while` loop that takes the following form:

```
do {
    statement
} while(expression);
```

The main difference between the two is that execution is guaranteed at least once with the `do ... while` loop. The following example illustrates this:

```
do {
  console.log('This will print at least once');
}
while (false);
```

We use `while (false)` to emphasize that the `while` check terminates the loop. Nonetheless, there will still be a single print to the console. With a slight modification, our `while` example can be rewritten as its `do ... while` equivalent:

```
var tasksToDo = 3;

do {
  console.log('There are ' + tasksToDo + ' tasks to do');
  tasksToDo--;
}
while (tasksToDo > 0);
```

This code will result in exactly the same console output. For many problems, it is possible to use either a `while` or a `do ... while`, so the question becomes which one to choose. We would recommend `while` as the default choice, only using `do ... while` on those occasions when a statement has to be executed at least once.

The `for` Loop

The `for` loop is used to run a code block a number of times, and is often referred to as a counting loop. It takes this general form:

```
for (initialization; condition; end-expression ) {
  statement
}
```

As a simple example, consider the following:

```
for (var i = 0; i < 3; i++) {
  console.log(i);
}
```

The above loop will declare the variable i and assign it the initial value of 0. On each iteration, i will be outputted and then incremented by 1. It is important to

note that the variable is both declared and initialized. It's syntactically valid to omit
the declaration:

```
for (i = 0; i < 3; i++) {
   console.log(i);
}
```

However, this will create a global variable, i, which is undesirable. It will potentially
clash with other variables of the same name, and could lead to memory leaks as
well as a host of other disagreeable phenomena. If you are creating a new variable
at the beginning of your for loop, always remember the var! A for loop can also
have multiple tests:

```
for (var i = 0; i < 10 && i % 2 === 0; i+=4) {
   console.log(i);
}
```

Here we're testing that i is less than 10 and divisible by 2, which will print:

```
0
4
8
```

It's also possible to have multiple initializations and end expressions:

```
for (var i = 0, j = 0; i < 3; i++, j+=2) {
   console.log(i, j);
}
```

Before running the code, try to work out what it will print to the console. Did you
guess the following correctly?

```
0 0
1 2
2 4
```

The loop is running two end expressions and so, on each iteration, i is being incremented by 1 and j is being incremented by 2. Note also that while the end expression
is generally used to increment a counter, it can take on any number of forms. For

example, we could assign i to be a random number using the built in `Math.random()` function:

```
for (var i = 0; i < 0.9; i = Math.random()) {
  console.log(i);
}
```

Here the loop will keep on iterating until the random number generator produces a value of 0.9 or greater. As you can see, the `for` loop is a powerful and flexible construct, and is likely to be the one you'll use the most.

The for ... in Loop

The `for ... in` loop was covered in the last chapter. To recap, this statement is used to loop through the properties of an object; for example:

for-in.html (excerpt)

```
var agents = {
  '005': "Michael Harp",
  '006': "John Smith",
  '007': "James Bond"
};

for (key in agents) {
    if ('007' === key) {
        console.log('Bond, ' + agents[key] + '
➥has been found!');
    } else {
        console.log('Standard spy, ' + agents[key] + '
➥has been found');
    }
}
```

There are a few important points worth keeping in mind. First, avoid using this with arrays; instead, use the standard `for` loop. Second, do not rely on the loop returning objects in the same order in which they were defined. Although most vendors do implement the loop in this way, it's not actually part of the specification, so there's potential a standards-compliant vendor may decide on a different implementation.

Jumps

Broadly speaking, a jump statement is used to move to another part of the script. The jump statements in JavaScript are break, continue, labeled statements, and return. return is used for exiting functions, while the rest are used with loops. Let's break this down in detail.

break

The break statement is used to exit from a loop. Suppose we wish to iterate through the task list and stop once we've hit the first completed a task. This could be accomplished with a break statement:

break.html (excerpt)

```
var tasks = [
  {name: 'Buy milk', complete: false},
  {name: 'Trash', complete: false},
  {name: 'Pay bills', complete: true},
  {name: 'Repairs', complete: false},
  {name: 'Plumber', complete: true}
];
var firstComplete;

for (var i = 0; i < tasks.length; i++) {
  if (tasks[i].complete) {
    firstComplete = tasks[i];
    break;
  }
}

console.log(firstComplete);
```

Note that break is only used for exiting from loops. Do not use it to try to exit from conditionals such as if. The previous example can be refactored to be written without the break:

```
for (var i = 0; i < tasks.length && firstComplete ===
➥undefined; i++) {
    if (tasks[i].complete) {
```

```
      firstComplete = tasks[i];
    }
  }
```

From the start, the reader can see that the loop is meant to exit once `firstComplete` is assigned a value. When using `break`, it is almost always possible to replace it using conditional statements, so it's worth considering which option is cleaner and clearer before writing your code. As a practical guideline, if your `break` statement is going to be deeply buried within the middle of a loop, consider ways of either bringing it to the top or refactoring to avoid it entirely.

continue

The `continue` statement is also used in the context of loops; however, instead of breaking from the loop, it skips to the next iteration. In a `while` loop, this means that the condition is tested again. In a `for` loop, the end expression is run and then the loop continues. Assuming the same `tasks` variable from the previous example, let's look at an example:

continue.html (excerpt)

```
for (var i = 0; i < tasks.length; i++) {
  if (!tasks[i].complete) {
    continue;
  }

  console.log(i, tasks[i].name);
}
```

This code prints the tasks that are complete, yielding this:

```
2 'Pay bills'
4 'Plumber'
```

We choose to print the value of the counter `i` to demonstrate the effect of using `continue` on counter incrementation. Notice how it causes the loop to continue, as well as running the end condition to increment the counter. Let's revisit our simple `while` example. Suppose we wish to skip the case when `tasksToDo` is equal to 2. Without typing in the code, consider whether this solution would work:

```
var tasksToDo = 3;

while (tasksToDo > 0) {
  if (tasksToDo == 2) {
    continue;
  }

  console.log('There are ' + tasksToDo + ' tasks to do');
  tasksToDo--;
}
```

Did you spot the error? By continuing, we bypass tasksToDo—and become stuck in an infinite loop. We'll leave it as an exercise for you to fix the example using a conditional and then compare the two pieces of code for clarity. It is easier for our brains to process in a linear manner. More cognitive overhead is needed to process jump statements, making it more likely for mistakes to creep into our code. It's up to the programmer to decide on whether a particular method maximizes clarity and readability; in this sense, programming is as much an art as it is a science.

Labeled Statements

Labeled statements are used in conjunction with break and continue. A statement can be labeled by prefixing it with an identifier:

```
identifier: statement
```

Let's look at an example from the Mozilla Developer Network[3], which actually comes with a warning: "As much as possible, avoid using labels and, depending on the cases, prefer calling functions or throwing an error." When code comes with a warning, take note! Their example is as follows:

labeled-statements.html (excerpt)

```
var i, j;

loop1:
for (i = 0; i < 3; i++) {
➥//The first for statement is labeled "loop1"
  loop2:
```

---

[3] https://developer.mozilla.org/en-US/docs/JavaScript/Reference/Statements/label

```
        for (j = 0; j < 3; j++) {
//The second for statement is labeled "loop2"
            if (i == 1 && j == 1) {
                continue loop1;
            } else {
                console.log("i = " + i + ", j = " + j);
            }
        }
    }
```

Before running this code, guess what it will do, and see if the result matches your expectations:

```
i = 0, j = 0
i = 0, j = 1
i = 0, j = 2
i = 1, j = 0
i = 2, j = 0
i = 2, j = 1
i = 2, j = 2
```

The key to understanding this code is analyzing `continue loop1;`. When i and j are both equal to 1, the `continue` is executed, at which point the code jumps back to the labelled `loop1`, the counter i is incremented, and execution resumes. Even this basic example can be rather confusing, though it can be written to be shorter and clearer without the labeled statement:

```
for (var i = 0; i < 3; i++) {
  for (j = 0; j < 3; j++) {
    var invalid = i == 1 && j >= 1;

    if (!invalid) {
      console.log("i = " + i + ", j = " + j);
    }
  }
}
```

Although there are times when you may use `break` and `continue`, you will almost never need to use labeled statements in practice. However, if you now come across it in a programmer's code, you'll no longer wonder what the code is doing, although you may perhaps question what the original coder was thinking!

return

`return` is the most commonly used jumping statement. It takes the following general form:

```
return expression;
```

or less commonly:

```
return;
```

It can only be used within a function, and is used to delineate the return value of a function. If the expression is omitted, the return value is undefined. For a simple example:

```
function divideBy(numerator, denominator) {
    return numerator / denominator;
}
```

The more observant among you will note that, depending on how this function is used, we have a potential "divide by zero" problem. Syntactically, it's possible to have any number of `return` statements in a given function. As a matter of good practice, we recommend erring toward a single `return` statement per function. This so-called single point of exit makes the code more understandable and easier to debug. In a debugger, it's only necessary to monitor one statement instead of two or more.

 On Division by Zero

JavaScript is unusual among programming languages in that dividing by zero doesn't naturally cause an exception in the language. A positive number divided by zero yields infinity. A negative number divided by zero yields - infinity. Zero divided by zero yields `NaN`. In all cases, normal execution of the program can continue. However, we still need to deal with the "division by zero" issue.

For example, suppose you wish to calculate a user's body mass index (BMI). This is given by the formula: weight / (height x height). If the height comes into the function with a value of zero, there is a good argument for raising an exception.

> Users may not take to it kindly if you tell them they have a BMI of infinity! Such
> a number may also cause problems with downstream applications, such as charts.

There are cases when multiple `return` statements will make the code easier to read.
Suppose we wish to merge two task lists. Using a single exit point, we could write
the code this way:

```javascript
function mergeTasks(taskList1, taskList2) {
  var merged;

  if (taskList1 === undefined)
    merged = taskList2;
  else if (taskList2 === undefined)
    merged = taskList1;
  else {
    // merge code
    merged = ...;
  }

  return merged;
}
```

With multiple exit points, the code can be written in a slightly cleaner manner:

```javascript
function mergeTasks(taskList1, taskList2) {
  if (taskList1 === undefined) {
    return taskList2;
  } else if (taskList2 === undefined) {
    return taskList1;
  }

  // merge code
  var merged = ...;
  return merged
}
```

Note how in the second example we have "guard" statements to check for exception
conditions, followed by a single exit at the end. As a practical guideline, it is fine
to follow this pattern of guard statements at the top followed by a single exit. It's
when we have `return` statements cropping up in the middle of long functions that
code potentially becomes more difficult to understand and maintain.

Exception Handling

JavaScript provides a mechanism to handle exceptional circumstances by transferring control to special error-handling sections of the code. To catch exceptions, we must place the potentially offending code within a `try` block. When an error occurs, an exception is thrown and control is transferred to code within the `catch` block. If no exception is thrown, the exception handler is ignored and the code continues as normal. This will be explained in more detail shortly.

throw

The keyword `throw` is used to signal an error condition. It takes this form:

```
throw expression;
```

While it is syntactically valid to throw an exception this way:

```
throw "This is an error in the form of a string";
```

the preferred format is to explicitly use an `Error` object. Continuing with the example from the prior section:

```
function divideBy(numerator, denominator) {
  if (denominator === 0) {
    throw new Error('Denominator must be non zero');
  }

  return numerator / denominator;
}
```

An `Error` object provides more information than a string. It is possible for upstream functions to specifically test if an object is an error by using `instanceof Error`. As to the question of what we do once we throw an error, we'll look to the next section.

try

The previously mentioned `try` statement assumes the following form:

```
try {
    // code which may throw an error
} catch (identifier) {
    // error handling
} finally {
    // clean up code
}
```

The `try` clause encloses a block of code in which an exception can occur, while the `catch` clause provides the exception handling. The `finally` clause is optional; if present, it always executes and is generally used to perform a clean-up. Using the same `divideBy` function from the previous section, here's an example in which no error condition is generated:

```
try {
    var result = divideBy(7, 2);

    console.log(result);
} catch (e) {
    console.log(e.message);
} finally {
    console.log('This will always execute');
}
```

Note that the code inside the `finally` clause executes, even though there's no error. Now for an example that will throw an error:

```
try {
    divideBy(7, 0);
    console.log(result);
} catch (e) {
    console.log(e.message);
} finally {
    console.log('This will always execute');
}
```

Note that `console.log(result);` is no longer executed; the code jumps straight to the `catch` clause. At this point, it prints the error message and then moves to the `finally` clause as before.

An Empirical Study

There is some vigorous debate in the programming community as to whether certain jump statements constitute bad practice. For example, Douglas Crockford, author of *JavaScript: The Good Parts*,[4] recommends to "avoid use of the `continue` statement. It tends to obscure the control flow of the function."[5]

Rather than wade into the debate, we've taken the liberty of conducting an empirical study using jQuery, one of the most well-known and popular JavaScript libraries. If your operating system supports `wget`, `grep`, and `wc`, you can try it yourself; otherwise, follow along with the text. First, download the uncompressed version of the code:

```
wget http://code.jquery.com/jquery-1.9.1.js
```

Use a combination of `grep` and word count to see how many times `break` is used:

```
> grep 'break;' jquery-1.9.1.js | wc -l
> 16
```

Similarly, we check for `continue`:

```
> grep 'continue;' jquery-1.9.1.js | wc -l
> 7
```

`function`:

```
> grep 'function' jquery-1.9.1.js | wc -l
> 624
```

and `return`:

```
> grep 'return' jquery-1.9.1.js | wc -l
> 646
```

---

[4] http://shop.oreilly.com/product/9780596517748.do?CMP=OTC-KW7501011010&ATT=9780596517748
[5] http://javascript.crockford.com/code.html

So, to summarize, across a code base spanning nearly 10,000 lines and some 600 functions and `return` statements, `break` is used 16 times and `continue` is used 7 times. I'll let you draw your own conclusions from the data.

Loop Alternatives

On Style

Syntactically, JavaScript takes its syntax from Java, which in turn takes its syntax from C. In both of these languages, `for` and `while` loops feature prominently. However, the official specification discusses how in terms of programming philosophy JavaScript actually takes its major ideas from Self and Scheme.[6]

Scheme is a functional programming language, and if we look at some documentation on its syntax,[7] we observe: "Scheme is very odd in one sense, it has no expressions designed for looping, repeating, or otherwise doing something more than once at a general level." JavaScript takes major ideas from a language with no expressions for loops! How can this be? Let's now have a look at some of the alternatives to loops.

Higher Order Functions

Earlier in the text, we briefly touched on the newer built-in array iteration functions: `forEach`, `every`, `some`, `filter`, `map`, `reduce`, and `reduceRight`. These are higher order functions because they accept functions as their arguments. They can be used instead of loops to facilitate programming in a more functional style. For example, suppose we have an array and we wish to add up the even numbers:

```
var myNums = [3, 5, 10, 4, 2, 1, 16, 7];
```

Using a loop-based approach would yield a similar result to this:

```
var sum = 0;

for (var i = 0; i < myNums.length; i++) {
  if (myNums[i] % 2 === 0) {
```

---

[6] http://www.ecmascript.org/es4/spec/overview.pdf
[7] http://en.wikibooks.org/wiki/Scheme_Programming/Looping

```
        sum += myNums[i];
    }
  }

  console.log(sum);
```

There is nothing complicated in this; we're using plain vanilla loops as has been explained throughout the chapter. Using a functional approach would produce the following:

```
var sum = myNums.filter(function(x) {
    return x % 2 === 0
}).reduce(function(num1, num2) {
    return num1 + num2;
})

console.log(sum);
```

Here we're using `filter` to extract only the even-numbered values; then we are using `reduce` to add up the list. Same result, but nary a loop in sight. Let's look at a to-do list example, where we have a bunch of tasks with a bunch of owners; we wish to transfer the tasks of Paul and James to poor David:

```
var tasks = [
    {name: 'Buy milk', owner: 'James'},
    {name: 'Trash', owner: 'Jill'},
    {name: 'Bills', owner: 'Paul'},
    {name: 'Repairs', owner: 'Jill'},
    {name: 'Plumber', owner: 'James'}
];
```

Here's one way of doing this is:

```
var numTasks = 0;
var newTasks = [];

for (var i = 0; i < tasks.length; i++) {
  var task = tasks[i];

  if (task.owner === 'Paul' || task.owner === 'James') {
    var newTask = {name: task.name, owner: 'David'};
```

```
        newTasks.push(newTask);
    }
}

console.log(newTasks);
```

Here we are checking for the specified names, creating a new task, and then pushing it into a new array. A more functional style would be:

```
var newTasks = tasks.filter(function(task) {
    return task.owner === 'Paul' || task.owner === 'James'
}).map(function(t) {
    t.owner = 'David';

    return t;
});

console.log(newTasks);
```

Here we use a `filter` to create an array with only the specified owners; then we map the tasks to the new owner. For our next example, we wish to count the number of tasks that have been assigned to a particular person. Here is where the elegance of functional programming can truly shine. The imperative way is to go through each task and increment a counter as follows:

```
var tasks = [
    {name: 'Buy milk', owner: 'James'},
    {name: 'Trash', owner: 'Jill'},
    {name: 'Bills', owner: 'Paul'},
    {name: 'Repairs', owner: 'Jill'},
    {name: 'Plumber', owner: 'James'}
];

function countByOwner(tasks, name) {
    var count = 0;

    for (var i = 0; i < tasks.length; i++) {
        if (tasks[i].owner === name) {
            count++;
        }
    }
```

```
        return count;
    }

    console.log(countByOwner(tasks, 'James'));
```

The functional way is to filter for the owner and then check the length of the array:

```
    function countByOwner(tasks, name) {
      return tasks.filter(function(task) {
        return task.owner === name;
      }).length;
    }
```

The functional mindset in some ways is less intuitive than the imperative one; however, as demonstrated, it can be used to clearly and elegantly express a solution that would take an imperative program many more lines to accomplish.

Recursion

Let's briefly touch on the concept of recursion. Many functional approaches eschew loops in favor of recursion. The following example will illustrate. Remember from high school calculating the factorial of a number? Without going into the formal definition, we'll just use this simple example: 5 factorial is 5 x 4 x 3 x 2 x 1, which is 120. Here's the factorial function with loops:

```
    function factorial(num) {
      var result = 1;

      for (var i = num; i > 0; i--) {
        result *= i;
      }

      return result;
    }
```

Alternatively, we can implement a recursive function that calls itself:

```
    function factorial(num) {
      if (1 === num) {
        return num;
```

```
        } else {
            return num * factorial(num - 1);
        }
    }
```

Many problems lend themselves to elegant recursive solutions. Recursion is a fairly involved computer science topic, but if you start keeping an eye out for that loops can be refactored as recursions, the number of instances where they naturally occur may surprise you.

For those of you who wish to explore recursion in greater depth, Kirit Sælensminde's "Recursive Rights and Wrongs" article will prove useful.[8] It touches upon important topics beyond the scope of this book, such as performance considerations.

Project

Counting Tasks

Suppose we wish to count the number of tasks that have been completed. We'll need this functionality later when we provide charts. Using loops, one way of completing the task would be as follows:

```
function countComplete(tasks) {
    var numCompleted = 0;

    for (var i = 0; i < tasks.length; i++) {
        if (tasks[i].complete) {
            numCompleted++;
        }
    }

    return numCompleted;
}
```

All in all, this is a reasonable approach. The logic is simple enough, and we have a counter to track the number of tasks completed. We then loop through our task list and every time we see a completed item, we increment the counter. Is there a

---

[8] http://www.kirit.com/Recursive%20rights%20and%20wrongs

better solution? Yes. Functional programming to the rescue! Place this code into a file named **todo.js**:

```
function countComplete(tasks) {
  return tasks.filter(function(task) {
    return task.complete;
  }).length;
}
```

Now all we have to do is filter the entire list based on whether a task is complete, and then return the length of that list.

Sorting

We want to provide our users with the ability to sort by three criteria: low-to-high, high-to-low, and name. Thanks to the built-in `sort` function, all we have to do is provide a function to rank our tasks based on the specified criterion:

```
var sortByLowHigh = function(tasks) {
  return tasks.sort(function(task1, task2) {
    return task2.priority - task1.priority;
  });
};

var sortByHighLow = function(tasks) {
  return tasks.sort(function(task1, task2) {
    return task1.priority - task2.priority;
  });
};

var sortByName = function(tasks) {
  return tasks.sort(function(task1, task2) {
    return task1.text > task2.text;
  });
};
```

For priority sorting, we compare the tasks numerically. For name sorting, we compare lexicographically. For the curious, the built-in array-sorting function uses an algorithm internally known as QuickSort.[9]

---

[9] http://www.nczonline.net/blog/2012/11/27/computer-science-in-javascript-quicksort/

Summary

We have covered a lot of ground in this chapter. We started by taking a look at loops, including `while`, `do ... while`, `for`, and `for ... in`. We then moved onto jumps, including labeled statements, `break`, `continue`, and `return`. We also discussed exception handling, using `throw` and `try ... catch ... finally` before moving on to talking about higher order functions and how they're used to implement functional programming solutions. Finally, we took a quick look at recursion, and how it can elegantly replace loops in certain solutions.

By now, you'll have a firm grasp of loops and jumps, and are beginning to gain insights into cases where functional solutions can concisely replace their imperative counterparts.

The Document Object Model

What is the DOM?

The Document Object Model (DOM) is an API for manipulating HTML and XML documents. It's a tree hierarchy of objects representing a document, and facilitates scripting by exposing methods and properties. Though the DOM is quite powerful today, and large parts of its specification are well-supported across all major browsers, this wasn't always the case.

At first there was little uniformity, let alone a specification. Back in the bad old days of the Browser Wars,[1] when Netscape and Microsoft were vying for supremacy over the Web, one-upmanship was the name of the game. This lead to conflicting implementations, with each manufacturer introducing non-standard features into its own product. As developers began using these features, competing vendors were forced to mimic the behavior so that web pages wouldn't break in their own browsers. Features were forced into existence simply by whoever held significant market share with their browser. As you can imagine, it was a headache at best for web developers trying to make their code work in the major browsers of the day.

[1] http://en.wikipedia.org/wiki/Browser_wars

In 1997, the World Wide Web Consortium (W3C) standardized the DOM with the release of DOM Level 1, or DOM1.[2] It would continue this process through DOM2, DOM3, and most recently DOM4, which we'll cover in more detail later. Once the W3C introduced DOM1, all previous incarnations of the DOM became referred to as the Legacy DOM, DOM Level 0, or DOM0.[3]

The Need for Backward Compatibility

The web is a strange animal, unlike any other software. Though browsers continue to evolve, the pages that they interpret can date from as far back as 1991. This means that any innovation or iteration on existing browser technology must continue to work with older web pages. It's because of this phenomenon that the DOM as we know it today contains artifacts from the "bad old days."

The document Object

The document object is a top-level object encompassing (and acting as an entry point into) your document. All the objects, methods, and properties that you'll need to work with your document hang off the document object. For example, one of the most common methods in use today is getElementById, which returns an element in the DOM by its id attribute:

getElementById.html (excerpt)

```
<!doctype html>
<html>
<head>
</head>
<body>
  <div id="foo">Foo, baby. Foo!</div>
  <div id="bar">Meh.</div>
  <script>
    // returns a reference to the first div
    var el = document.getElementById("foo");
  </script>
</body>
</html>
```

---

[2] http://en.wikipedia.org/wiki/Document_Object_Model#Standardization

[3] http://en.wikipedia.org/wiki/Document_Object_Model#Legacy_DOM

You can also retrieve other information, such as the document's title, simply by using `document.title`.

DOM Level 0 or Legacy DOM

A few throwbacks to the days of the Legacy DOM are the document's `forms`, `links`, and `images` collections. This practice of providing named accessors for specific element types was discontinued in DOM Level 1. In DOM0, however, this was how you accessed `<form>`, `<image>`, and `<anchor>` elements. You could do this by using either the name of the element, or passing its index into the appropriate accessor via the `document` object. Let's take the following document, for example:

```
<html>
<head>
</head>
<body>
  <img src="mom.jpg" name="mother">
  <img src="dad.jpg" name="father">
  <form name="contact">
    <a href="http://www.sitepoint.com" name="sitepoint">
➥ SitePoint </a>
  </form>
  <a href="http://www.w3.org" name="w3">W3C</a>
  <script>
    var mom, dad, sitepoint, contact;

    mom = document.images.mother; dad = document.images[1];
    sitepoint = document.links.sitepoint;
    contact = document.contact;
  </script>
</body>
</html>
```

The resulting DOM hierarchy is seen in Figure 6.1.

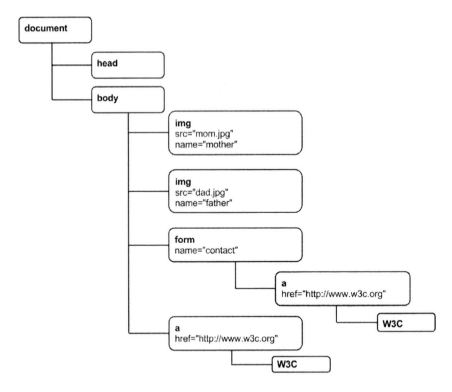

Figure 6.1. DOM0 hierarchy

You could access the form named `contact` by using `document.contact`. You could also access it by using `document.forms[0]`, assuming the form you wanted was the first one in the page's hierarchy (which, in this case, it is). If it were the second of two forms, you'd use `document.forms[1]`, and so on. In our example, we access the second image by referring to `document.images[1]`. This syntax can be used for all three accessors. As with any array, you can loop over the returned results:

```
var imgs, img, i;

imgs = document.images;

for (i = 0; i < imgs.length; i += 1) {
  ing = imgs[i]; // get reference to image element
  console.log(img);
}
```

DOM Level 1

In 1998, the W3C released the DOM Level 1 specification.[4] The spec took the existing hierarchy of the DOM and normalized its contents by introducing the Node object, from which most objects are derived. Of the handful of object types that the specification added, the most common are Document, Element, Attr, and Text, which account for the majority of the contents of an HTML document.

In the following HTML, the <div> will become an Element node, its id attribute will become an Attr node, and the "Hello!" will become a Text node:

```
<html>
<head>
</head>
<body>
  <div id="welcome">Hello!</div>
</body>
</html>
```

The previously mentioned Document node is actually an abstract node that wraps everything, and doesn't directly represent any tags in the HTML. The <html> tag is a special Element node, known as the document element, and can be accessed at document.documentElement.

There are also less common types of nodes such as ProcessingInstruction and EntityReference, but we'll stick to the most common ones for our purposes. A listing of the various node types is shown in Figure 6.2.

---

[4] http://www.w3.org/TR/REC-DOM-Level-1/

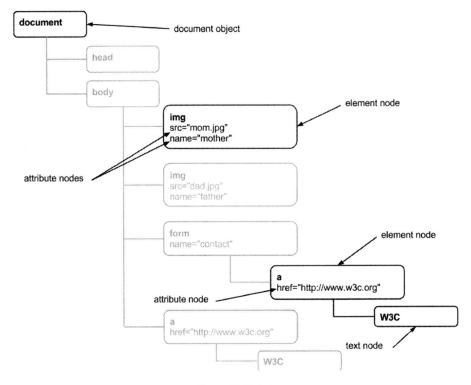

Figure 6.2. Node types

Creating DOM Elements and Attributes

At the root of our DOM tree is the document element, and there can only be one per document. Since it encompasses the rest of the document's nodes, it has a set of methods allowing you to create all the child nodes that it can contain. So if you wanted to create a `<div>` element, for example, you'd use the `document` object's `createElement` method in this way:

```
var myDiv = document.createElement("div");
```

This returns an empty `<div>` element. It's important to note that the element we've just created currently only exists in memory, and is not part of the document. In order to add our `<div>` to the document, we need to append it to a node somewhere in the DOM using the `appendChild` method.

Remember when we said that all objects derive from `Node`? Well, since `Node` exposes the `appendChild` method, we can use that method to append our newly created

`<div>` as a child of any given object in the DOM. Let's add our `<div>` to the contact form in the previous DOM0 example. We can still access our contact form by its name attribute, so let's just call `appendChild` off it to add our `<div>` to the form:

```
var myDiv = document.createElement("div");

document.contact.appendChild(myDiv);
```

Our form now looks like this:

```
<form name="contact">
  <a href="http://www.sitepoint.com" name="sitepoint">
➥ SitePoint </a>
  <div></div>
</form>
```

Once we've added our `<div>`, we can add attributes using the `setAttribute` method. So, for example, we could give our `<div>` a name attribute:

```
var myDiv = document.createElement("div");

myDiv.setAttribute("name", "foo");
document.contact.appendChild(myDiv);
```

This will give us a `<div>`:

```
<div name="foo"></div>
```

It's important to note that all DOM object references are live. Even after we've added our `<div>` to the DOM, we can continue to work with it. In other words, it yields the same results:

```
var myDiv = document.createElement("div");

document.contact.appendChild(myDiv);
myDiv.setAttribute("name", "foo");
```

Additionally, if some other code were to modify our `<div>`, our reference held in `myDiv` would still be up to date. What's more, we can immediately reference our new `<div>` by its name, `foo`.

Though we can use `setAttribute` to set attributes on elements, we can also use `createAttribute` to create attribute nodes. Attributes also derive from the `Node` object, starting in the DOM1 spec:

```
var myLink, href;

myLink = document.createElement("a");
href = document.createAttribute("href");
href.nodeValue = "http://www.sitepoint.com/";
myLink.setAttributeNode(href);
```

We've created an anchor and an `href` attribute, to which we add a URL via its `nodeValue` property. Bear in mind that even though the `href` attribute object derives from `Node`, you're unable to append objects to it. Trying to do so will result in a `HierarchyRequestError: DOM Exception 3` error.

Now that we've created an anchor with an `href` attribute, we can add some text to make the link clickable. For this, we use `createTextNode` to add the text node to our link:

```
var myLink, href, linkText;

myLink = document.createElement("a");
href = document.createAttribute("href");
href.nodeValue = "http://www.sitepoint.com/";
myLink.setAttributeNode(href);
linkText = document.createTextNode("SitePoint");
myLink.appendChild(linkText);
```

Again, text nodes are like attribute nodes in that they're unable to have children.

 A Note on Nodes

Although all objects derive from `Node`, some are leaf nodes and others aren't. Text nodes are leaf nodes and therefore cannot have children. As a result, methods such as `childNodes` are inapplicable and cannot be used.

insertBefore

We've just seen `appendChild` in action, but sometimes we want to be more specific about where we insert an element, rather than just appending it at the end. That's where `insertBefore` comes in. As its name implies, it tells the DOM that you want to insert an element before another node that you specify:

insertBefore.html (excerpt)

```
var list, item1, item2, item3;

list = document.createElement("ul");
item1 = document.createElement("li");
item1.appendChild(document.createTextNode("1"));
item2 = document.createElement("li");
item2.appendChild(document.createTextNode("2"));
item3 = document.createElement("li");
item3.appendChild(document.createTextNode("3"));
list.appendChild(item1);
list.appendChild(item3);
list.insertBefore(item2, item3);
```

Here we've created a `<ul>` and three `<li>` elements. We've also added a number to each `<li>`. We then append the first and third items to our list. Finally, we use `insertBefore` to inject `item2` between `item1` and `item3`. The resulting DOM tree structure is:

```
<ul>
  <li>1</li>
  <li>2</li>
  <li>3</li>
</ul>
```

getElementsByTagName

In the Legacy DOM, you could access elements either directly by their name attribute values or by the specialized collections such as `document.forms` and `document.images`. Then DOM1 introduced the the more generic `getElementsByTagName` method. It's a method that you can use from `document`, or any object of type `Element`. For example, if you want all the anchors in a page, you can write `document.getElementsByTagName("a")`, which will return a collection of all the anchors in the document, regardless of where they're located in the DOM's hierarchy. You can also narrow down your lookup by using `getElementsByTagName` from a given element. So, if you had a form whose buttons you wanted to access, you could write `myForm.getElementsByTagName("button")`.

It should be pointed out that what `getElementsByTagName` returns is actually a `NodeList`. For all intents and purposes, a `NodeList` behaves much like an array in that it's an ordered collection of nodes. The similarity ends there, though, as a `NodeList` has none of an array's methods. In other words, it's not possible to `sort`, `join`, or `reverse` a `NodeList`'s contents like you could an array's. What's more, a `NodeList` is live.

As mentioned earlier about `Nodes`, the contents of a `NodeList` always reflect the current state of the underlying DOM. If a `Node` is deleted, the `NodeList` reflects that without you having to go and retrieve the list again. Element nodes, of which the majority of a DOM's nodes are, have a few other methods you can use to work with them.

getAttribute

With `getAttribute`, you can read an attribute's value. Given `<div name="foo"></div>`, `myDiv.getAttribute("name")` will return `"foo"`.

removeAttribute

You can completely remove an attribute from an element using `removeAttribute`. This is done by passing in the attribute name you want removed. So, given `<div name="foo"></div>`, `myDiv.removeAttribute("name")` will leave the `<div>` as `<div></div>`. Note that `removeAttribute` returns no value.

setAttributeNode

We saw this one in action earlier. After having created a new attribute node with `createAttribute`, we can add it to an element using `setAttributeNode`:

```
var el, attr;

el = document.createElement("div");
attr = document.createAttribute("name");
attr.nodeValue = "foo";
el.setAttributeNode(attr);
```

It's important to remember the step where you assign a value to your attribute with the `nodeValue` property. Otherwise, instead of a `<div>` that looks like `<div name="foo"></div>`, you'll end up with `<div name></div>`.

removeAttributeNode

Just as with `removeAttribute`, `removeAttributeNode` can be used to remove an attribute from an element. The difference with `removeAttributeNode` is that you need to pass in a reference to the attribute node that you want removed. In the case of our recent example, we'd do the following:

```
var el, attr;

el = document.createElement("div");
attr = document.createAttribute("name");
attr.nodeValue = "foo";
el.setAttributeNode(attr);
el.removeAttributeNode(attr);
```

DOM Level 2

The second iteration of the W3C's DOM[5] specification came out with a lot of namespace-friendly versions of existing DOM methods. This was to accommodate namespacing in XML documents. As mentioned at the start of this chapter, the DOM is designed to work with both HTML and XML, and since the W3C saw XML as the next logical step in HTML's evolution, it began to augment the DOM with XML-friendly features.

Since we're only concerned with the HTML DOM in this book, we can ignore them. The only noteworthy additions to the DOM in DOM2, therefore, are `getElementById`, `hasAttributes`, and `hasAttribute`.

getElementById

This addition to the DOM is fairly significant, as it allows the targeting of an element in a document with a unique `id` value. If no `id`s match, `null` is returned. Otherwise, a reference to the element with the matching `id` value is returned.

 On Uniqueness

The part about the `id` being unique is important. If your document contains more than one element with the same identifier, `getElementById` will more than

---

[5] http://www.w3.org/TR/DOM-Level-2-Core/

likely only return the first element that matches it. However, because the specification doesn't state what the behavior should be in such a scenario, you could receive unpredictable results depending on the implementation. For this reason, always make sure that `ids` in a document are unique.

Given `<div id="foo"></div>`, `document.getElementById("foo")` will return that `<div>` element.

hasAttributes

If you need to know if a given element has any attributes attached to it, you can use `hasAttributes`. The method responds with a Boolean value, where `true` indicates the presence of attributes, and `false` shows otherwise.

hasAttribute

If you want to check for the existence of a particular attribute, use `hasAttribute`. It also returns a Boolean value. `true` is returned if the attribute you're looking for exists, while `false` indicates that it doesn't. Therefore, given `<div id="foo"></div>`, `myDiv.hasAttribute("id")` will return `true`, while `myDiv.hasAttribute("name")` will return `false`.

DOM Level 3

A bunch of new attributes and methods were specified in the DOM Level 3 specification, but none of them are particularly useful for day-to-day web development, nor are they broadly implemented. What's more, a majority of them concern themselves with the XML DOM.

A couple you may find interesting are the `textContent` attribute and the `isEqualNode` method.

Given the HTML `<p id="greeting"></p>`, its text content can be set to the string `"Good morning!"`:

```
var el = document.getElementById("greeting");

el.textContent = "Good morning!";
```

You have to be careful, though, because it will overwrite all the target element's contents, including any child elements.

With `isEqualNode`, you can compare to see if two nodes are identical. So, comparing two blank `<div>` elements will return `true`; however, if one of the `<div>`s had a class name, it would return `false`:

isEqualNode.html (excerpt)

```
var div1, div2, div3;

div1 = document.createElement("div");
div2 = document.createElement("div");
div3 = document.createElement("div");
div3.className = "chocolate";
div1.isEqualNode(div2); // returns true
div1.isEqualNode(div3); // returns false
```

DOM Level 4

In 2004, the Web Hypertext Application Technology Working Group (WHATWG) was formed in response to the W3C's decision to abandon HTML in favor of XML-based technologies, as well as its slow development of web standards. With the participation of Apple, Mozilla, and Opera, WHATWG brought forth HTML5—a broad collection of technologies of which the updated DOM is a part. In 2007, the W3C joined the effort, forking a copy of the specification and publishing it on its site under copyright.

The partnership between WHATWG and the W3C ended in 2011 when the latter wanted to publish a finished version of the spec (with known problems), while the WHATWG wanted to work on it as a "living standard," continually maintaining it. The most notable additions to DOM4 are `getElementsByClassName`, `prepend`, `append`, `before`, `after`, `replace`, and `remove`. As of this writing, all but `getElementsByClassName` are yet to be implemented in major browsers.

getElementsByClassName

Having native support for `getElementsByClassName` was a long time coming. For years, JavaScript libraries had filled the gap by providing non-native support for this missing feature. Now, however, you can perform this operation natively via

the DOM's API. As its name plainly states, you can now query the DOM for elements by their `class` values. You can use it directly from the `document` object `document.getElementsByClassName("report")`, which will return all elements in the document with the class name `report`. Or, you can narrow down your search by using the method from an element:
`document.getElementById("financials").getElementsByClassName("report")`.

Data Attributes

Although it was always possible to assign your own attributes to elements in the DOM, HTML5 codified the practice by introducing `data-*` attributes. If your application requires you to store data specific to an element, you can do it using a `data-*` attribute so that the data is stored directly with the element. This is advantageous over storing the data in an array/object because it's unnecessary to synchronize the DOM elements to the array/object in order to retrieve the data. Instead, you just retrieve the element from the DOM and read the `data-*` attribute's value directly from it.

A simple scenario where this could be useful is when displaying dates:

```
<span data-iso="1976-05-17T17:11:22">
➥DOB: May 17, 1976, 5:11 PM</span>
```

With an arrangement such as this, you can easily read the ISO format of a given date/time in the DOM without having to do any lookups in an array or any conversion of the human-readable format. Most modern browsers support the `dataset` accessor, which allows you to both set and get values from `data-*` attributes. For example, here's how we'd both set and read the value for our `<span>`:

```
        var el = document.createElement("span");

        el.appendChild(document.createTextNode
➥("DOB: May 17, 1976, 5:11 PM"));
        // setting the value
        el.dataset.iso = "1976-05-17T17:11:22";
        // reading the value
        el.dataset.iso; //returns "1976-05-17T17:11:22"
```

In this example, we create an element and assign a `data-iso` attribute to it. We also add its text content to be the human-readable format of the given date. This, of course, could just as easily have been rendered by the back end. In either case, reading the `data-iso` attribute is as simple as checking `.dataset.iso`.

The `style` Attribute

Back in DOM2, the W3C introduced the important and powerful `style` attribute (though plans for it were already being laid during work on DOM1). The `style` attribute allows for the programmatic manipulation of element styles. If you know CSS, using it is simple. Its format is simply `element.style.property = value` where `property` is a camel-case CSS property, and the value is the CSS value you'd assign in a regular stylesheet.

For example, given the HTML `<div id="hey">Hello, world!</div>`, the `<div>` style can be manipulated using the following JavaScript:

style.html (excerpt)

```
var myDiv = document.getElementById("hey");

myDiv.style.backgroundColor = "blue";
myDiv.style.border = "solid 5px #000";
myDiv.style.color = "#ffffff";
myDiv.style.padding = "20px 10px";
myDiv.style.margin = "2em";
myDiv.style.width = "200px";
```

The code will yield the style shown in Figure 6.3.

Figure 6.3. The style attribute

Project

In previous chapters, we looked at creating task objects and storing them in arrays and so on, but that's all very abstract. In order for users to be able to see their to-do list, we need to render the contents of our array to the screen. We've just looked at how to create DOM elements and add them to the document, so let's go ahead and write some code to do that:

```
var taskListForm, taskListEl;

taskListForm = document.getElementById("tasks");
taskListEl = taskListForm.getElementsByTagName("ul")[0];
```

First, we're obtaining references to both our `<form>` element as well as our `<ul>` element, which will contain our list of tasks. Now, let's write a function that will clear out our task list before we try to add anything to it. That way, we'll always have a clean slate with which to work:

```
function clearList() {
  while (taskListEl.hasChildNodes()) {
    taskListEl.removeChild(taskListEl.lastChild);
  }
}
```

We use a `while` loop to keep removing child nodes from our `taskListEl` until it's empty (and `hasChildNodes` returns `false`). Now we need a way to generate our task element. The HTML for it is this:

```
<li class="template-item">
  <input type="checkbox" >
  <span class="task-text label"></span>
  <input type="button" class="btn btn-mini delete-task"
➥value="Delete" >
  <div class="btn-group">
    <button class="btn btn-mini dropdown-toggle"
➥data-toggle="dropdown">
      Priority <span class="caret"></span>
    </button>
    <ul class="dropdown-menu">
      <li>
        <a href="#" class="highpriority" value="1">High</a>
      </li>
      <li>
        <a href="#" class="normalpriority" value="2">
➥Normal</a>
      </li>
```

```
      <li>
        <a href="#" class="lowpriority" value="3">Low</a>
      </li>
    </ul>
  </div>
</li>
```

As you can see, it's not just a matter of creating a simple `<li>` element. Instead of manually creating every element, attribute, and text node required for just one task item, why not use the DOM to our advantage and merely clone a node whenever we need it?

You'll note that we've gone ahead and given the `<li>` a class name of `"template-item"`. We'll use this to obtain the element and then clone it using the DOM's `cloneNode` method. We'll then fill in values specific to our task and have the function return the complete set of task elements so that it can be inserted into the DOM:

```
    function newRow(index, task) {
      var template, newRow, textEl;

      template = document.getElementsByClassName
➡ ("template-item")[0];
      newRow = template.cloneNode(true);
      newRow.setAttribute("data-idx", index.toString());

      // get task text el
      textEl = newRow.getElementsByClassName("task-text")[0];

      // set task priority
      if (task.priority == HIGHPRIORITY) {
        textEl.className += "label-important";
      } else if (task.priority == LOWPRIORITY) {
        textEl.className += " label-success";
      }

      // set task text
      textEl.appendChild(document.createTextNode(task.text));

      // mark complete
      if (task.complete) {
        newRow.getElementsByTagName("input")[0].setAttribute
```

```
➤("checked", "checked");
        newRow.getElementsByTagName("span")[0].className
➤+= "complete";
        }

    newRow.className = "task";

    return newRow;
    }
```

Once we have our template, the first task is to clone it with `cloneNode`. Notice how we're passing a value of `true` to `cloneNode`. This tells it that we want a deep clone rather than a shallow one. In other words, we want it to give us a copy of all the child nodes as well. Note also that the cloned node is only in memory and not part of the DOM. It will have to be inserted into the DOM once we're done working with it.

The next task is to add a `data-*` attribute so as to be able to match the task in the DOM with the one in our array. We do this by assigning a `data-idx` attribute and assigning it the index of the task in the array. We then get the element surrounding our task text and assign it a class name based on the task's priority, as well as create and append a text node containing the task's actual text (such as `"walk the dog"`).

Finally, if the task is complete, we check the checkbox and add a `"complete"` class name. We overwrite the `"template-item"` class name with `"task"`, and then return the DOM element (with child elements) to whomever called our function. Now all we have to do is call `clearList` and `newRow`:

```
var renderTaskList = function () {
    var i, task, taskEl;

    clearList();

    for (i = 0; i < tasks.length; i += 1) {
        task = tasks[i];
        taskEl = newRow(i, task);
        taskListEl.appendChild(taskEl);
    }
};
```

Here, we've created a `renderTaskList` function that, in order, clears the old list from the DOM by calling `clearList`, loops over our `tasks` array, calls `newRow`, takes its return value, and appends it to the DOM.

Summary

In this chapter, we took a look at the DOM—a hierarchical representation of the HTML document loaded into the browser. We saw how we can access its contents, as well as create new content to insert into it. We also saw how it's possible to manipulate the DOM's existing content and styles. The DOM's API is powerful and versatile, and harnessing it will allow any programmer the ability to build outstanding client-side applications.

Chapter

7

Events

This chapter is about JavaScript events. In order to provide interactivity, your application must be capable of processing input from the user. Due to the evolving nature of technology, the definition of what constitutes an event is in a constant state of flux. JavaScript came into existence in 1995. In those days people interacted with web pages almost exclusively using a keyboard and mouse. JavaScript events primarily consisted of plain vanilla human computer interactions such as: `keypress`, `mousedown`, `mouseup`, `click`, `scroll`, and `load`.

With the proliferation of smartphones, tablets and similar devices the number of events has increased dramatically. Nowadays aside from the basic keyboard and mouse events, APIs are available to detect orientation, zooming, and even humidity! This is functionality that did not exist just a few short years ago.

Rather than trying to cover the entire API with a broad sweeping brush, it would be more instructive to begin with a specific use case to illustrate some general ideas and concepts. Suppose you want to display an alert when a user clicks a button on a page. To process this event, it is necessary to answer a number of questions:

What was the action?   In this case it was a mouse click.

What part of the page received the action?   In this case it was a button.

How do we wish to handle the action?   Here we display an alert.

How do we specify a function to handle the action?   To answer this question, we need a way to simultaneously answer all of the previous questions.

While the above questions are somewhat of a simplification, they largely explain the JavaScript event model. Each step has its own formal description and definitions. Let's now look at each step of the process in detail.

DOM Events

To answer the question of "What was the action?", we turn to DOM events. There is no central authoritative specification available to define exactly what does and does not constitute an event. However, the Mozilla Developer Network provides a list of events[1].

This is not actually a specification. Rather, it is an amalgamation of a number of different specifications and provides a list of events along with a reference to the actual specification from which an event is derived. You will see that most of the events come from DOM Level 3 or HTML5. These APIs cover some of the more common cross-platform interactions such as keystrokes, mouseclicks, dragging, media, and offline behavior. However there are also some more obscure events such as `chargingchange`, which comes from the Battery Status API.

Not all events are universally supported across devices and browsers. For example, the Battery Status API is not supported in older versions of Internet Explorer. Additionally, while it may exist in desktop browsers, it is really only relevant in mobile devices such as laptops, tablets, and smartphones. We will be covering the main concepts and common use cases of events in this chapter. Once you have grasped the basics, you should be able to use the above reference to implement some of the more esoteric functionality if this is what your application requires.

---

[1] https://developer.mozilla.org/en-US/docs/DOM/Mozilla_event_reference

We have included some common events in Appendix A. Browsing through the list, you will notice that the `click` event is part of the DOM Level 3, and is fairly unambiguously described as "A pointing device button has been pressed and released on an element." You'll also notice that most other common events are DOM Level 3. Some of these events include `dblclick`, `mousedown`, `mouseup`, `keydown`, `keyup`, and `keypress`.

Event Propagation

Before turning to the question of "What part of the page received the action?", it is necessary to provide a brief overview of how events propagate through a page. Suppose you have a table and within that table you have an anchor tag. Both the table and the anchor tag have code to handle mouse clicks. When the user clicks on the anchor tag, which HTML element should process the event first? Should it be the table then the anchor tag or vice versa? To answer this question we must briefly explore the mechanics of event propagation.

In the early days, different browsers had different event-handling orders. Some would process the event by firing on the parent and then the child element, while others would do the opposite. In recent times, the W3C has begun to standardize event propagation in its DOM Level 3 document. The way an event travels through a document is captured diagrammatically as part of the DOM Level 3 Events Specification in Figure 7.1.

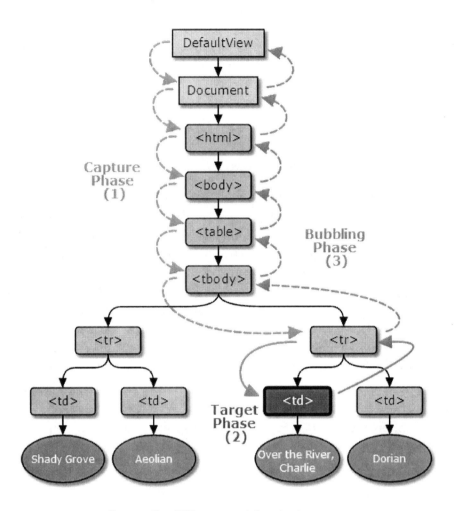

Figure 7.1. How DOM events travel through a document

Formally, the event path is broken into three phases. In the capture phase, the event starts at the top of the DOM tree, and propagates through to the parent of the target. In the target phase, the event object arrives at its target. This is generally where you will write your event-handling code. In the bubble phase, the event will move back up through the tree until it reaches the top. Bubble phase propagation happens in reverse order to the capture phase, with an event starting at the parent of the target and ending up back at the top of the DOM tree. These days, there's a choice to register an event in either the capture phase or the bubble phase. If you register an event in the capture phase, the parent element will process the event before the child element. In the above example, the table would process the event before the anchor. The opposite order will apply if bubbling is specified, in which case the child element will process the event before the parent. In our example, the anchor would receive the event before the table.

Note that specifying bubbling or capturing is optional, and is something that often does not even need to be considered. A conventional design would have each user action processed by only a single element. Only in unusual circumstances would a single action need to be processed by multiple elements concurrently. We include a brief discussion here because many of the event APIs make reference to capturing and bubbling, and it will be handy to understand what these terms mean. With some of the formal definitions out of the way we can now turn to making our pages actually respond to events!

Event Handlers

Normally you will want specific elements on your page to handle specific events. To indicate that a particular element on the page should process a particular event, you need to register an event handler on that element. There are three ways to register event handlers. To prepare us for the following sections create a new file named **events.html** containing the following HTML:

```
<!doctype html>
<html>
<head>
  <title>Events</title>
</head>
<body>
  <button>Click Me!</button>
</body>
</html>
```

This is a bare-bones page with a single button that we will use to process events.

HTML Attribute

It is possible to place JavaScript inline with your HTML. In the early days of JavaScript, this was the standard way of processing events. As an example, modify your `<button>` tag as follows:

```
<button onclick="alert('Old style event handling')">
➥Click Me!</button>
```

Now when you click on the button, you should see an alert similar to Figure 7.2.

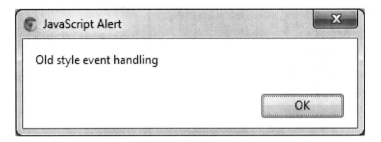

Figure 7.2. Inline JavaScript event handling

This method is not recommended. HTML should primarily be used as a presentation layer. JavaScript events are portions of business logic which make up the behavior layer. JavaScript code should not be mixed in with the presentation layer. Separating these two areas of your code will lead to greater maintainability.

addEventListener

The preferred way of handling events is by registering a handler via the function addEventListener. A handler can be thought of as a function that will process a particular event. addEventListener will register a single event handler on a target. Multiple event handlers can be added by calling this function multiple times. This function takes three parameters:

type   The event type we are listening for. In the case of a mouse click, it will be click.

listener   The listener, or handler, is the function that processes the event. In this case it will be our custom function that displays the alert.

useCapture If true, register the event handler for the capturing phase. If false, register the event handler for the bubbling phase. The default value is false.

Modify the HTML code to remove the inline JavaScript. Change the <button> tag to:

```
<button id="btnClickMe">Click Me!</button>
```

Then add a `<script>` tag just before the closing `</body>` tag:

```
<script src="events.js"></script>
```

Here we have removed the inline JavaScript and added an identifier so the button can be located by our JavaScript code. Next, create a new file named **events.js** containing the following code:

```
var myButton = document.getElementById("btnClickMe");

function handleClick() {
  alert("addEventListener clicked!");
}

myButton.addEventListener("click", handleClick, false);
```

Refresh the page, then click the button. You should now see the alert in Figure 7.3.

Figure 7.3. addEventListener event handling

Although it may seem like extra work, for any non-trivial project the separation of the presentation layer from the business logic will pay dividends. Under this architecture your designers can concentrate purely on the visual aspects and your JavaScript developers can concentrate purely on application logic without stepping on each other's feet.

 Internet Explorer

Before version 9, Internet Explorer did not support addEventListener. Instead it used its own proprietary mechanism. We won't cover the specifics of legacy

Internet Explorer methods, because it isn't the most productive use of our time;
should your application require support for older versions of this browser, we
recommend the use of a cross-browser library, such as jQuery.

DOM Element Properties

Another way of registering a handler is to simply set a property on the target itself.
The convention is to use on followed by the event name, in our case onclick. To
set onclick, replace all code in **events.js** as follows:

```
var myButton = document.getElementById("btnClickMe");

myButton.onclick = function(e) {
  alert("onclick click!");
};
```

You should see the alert in Figure 7.4 after refreshing the page and clicking the
button.

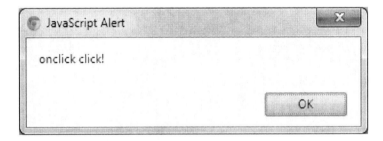

Figure 7.4. Using the onclick handler

Although setting a property directly on the element is simpler than
addEventListener, this comes at the cost of flexibility. Only one handler can be
added to an element using the on syntax. Suppose you wish to write code to interoperate with somebody else's code and you both wish to handle mouse clicks on
the same element: By setting DOM element properties directly, conflicts will arise
and ultimately only a single handler will be available to the user. The other handler
will be overriden. In contrast, by using addEventListener you could modify our
example as follows:

```
var myButton = document.getElementById("btnClickMe");

function handleClick() {
  alert("addEventListener clicked!");
}

function handleClick2() {
  alert("addEventListener2 clicked!");
}

myButton.addEventListener("click", handleClick, false);
myButton.addEventListener("click", handleClick2, false);
```

This would add multiple handlers for the single event. If you're curious, feel free to run the above code; you'll see that both handlers will fire and both alerts will display.

 Accessibility

There's a common saying that an escalator can never truly break because it can always function as a set of stairs. If your user's browser doesn't support JavaScript or some particular JavaScript function, where possible the design should be such that your users can still take the proverbial set of stairs. As a general rule this means that events should only be added to HTML elements that already have built-in behavior for that particular event. For example, click events should be applied to elements such as <a> and <button>. The majority of JavaScript events that you'll be dealing with have an HTML equivalent, and you should keep accessibility in mind when you design your page.

More Examples

Now that you understand the basics of event handlers, let's go through a few more examples to illustrate other events. You'll begin to notice a pattern that you'll be able to apply to just about any JavaScript event, whether or not we have specifically covered it in this chapter. Suppose we wish to determine when a page is loaded. Looking to Appendix A, we see the load event is defined as "A resource and its dependent resources have finished loading." We can detect when the page has loaded as follows:

```
window.onload = function(e) {
  alert("Page loaded");
};
```

Once you refresh the page you should see something similar to Figure 7.5.

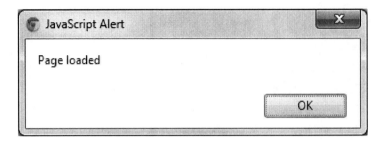

Figure 7.5. Determining when the page has loaded

It's very common in JavaScript to run code only after the page has finished loading. Often code will modify particular DOM elements. Therefore, it is necessary to ensure that these elements have been completely loaded before trying to access them. You can ensure this occurs by writing all of your code within the load event. Recall that in JavaScript it's perfectly legal to define functions within functions. Therefore, defining your application within a load event is perfectly valid.

Suppose now we wish to detect window resizes. By now, you should be familiar enough with events to be able to look up the name of the function and its description by yourself. The code to detect a resize looks like this:

```
window.onresize = function(e) {
  alert("Page resized");
};
```

When you resize the window you will notice that the alert fires:

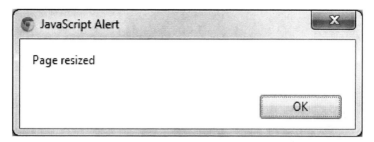

Figure 7.6. An alert is displayed when the window is resized

Depending on your browser, this event may fire twice! It would be remiss of us to discuss client-side JavaScript without briefly mentioning some of the perils and pitfalls, one of which you may have just seen. As a client-side JavaScript programmer, the reality is you will be dealing with many versions of JavaScript. Even within the same version of JavaScript, different browsers may have slightly different implementations of particular features. Although the most common functions should work in a uniform manner, occasionally you will run into an idiosyncrasies such as the above. Generally a library such as jQuery will help ease cross-browser issues, but we still strongly recommend familiarizing yourself with the material in this chapter so that even if you do end up using a cross-browser library, you will still understand what is happening under the hood.

 Why All the Quirks?

JavaScript's development as a programming language has followed a rather unique path. In a language such as C or Java, painstaking care is taken to ensure that programs behave as predictably as possible across a range of environments. In contrast, much of JavaScript's development occurred during the period of the so-called browser wars[2]. During this time vendors were not particularly concerned about interoperability with competing products. The legacy of this is a rather fragmented client-side JavaScript environment. The practical implication of all this is that when you write your client-side application, you will need to make a conscious decision about which browsers you are planning to support. According to best practices, you should try to support as many browsers as consistently as possible. You will need to test your application using each and every single browser to make sure that your program works as desired. As mentioned above, a library such as jQuery may make this problem much more tractable.

---

[2] http://en.wikipedia.org/wiki/Browser_wars

Event Context

Let's return to our very first click example:

```
var myButton = document.getElementById("btnClickMe");

myButton.onclick = function(e) {
  alert("onclick click!");
};
```

Suppose inside our event handler, we wish to know something about the HTML element that generated the event. This can be done by accessing `this`. Modify the function as follows:

```
myButton.onclick = function(e) {
  console.log(this);
};
```

When you refresh your page and click the button, the following should be displayed in the console:

```
<button id="btnClickMe">Click Me!</button>
```

Suppose instead we need information about the actual mouse click. In the above code, replace the logging statement with the following:

```
console.log(e);
```

Here, `e` represents the event object. When you next click on the button, you should see something like the following printed to the console:

```
MouseEvent {dataTransfer: null, toElement: button#btnClickMe,
➥fromElement: null, y: 41, x: 32...}
```

The event object contains all the properties of the mouse click. For example, suppose we are building a JavaScript video game and wish to track mouse movements. A simple logger could be created by adding the following code to **events.js**:

```
window.onmousemove = function(e) {
  console.log(e.x + ", " + e.y);
};
```

If you refresh your page and move your mouse around the screen, you should see something like Figure 7.7.

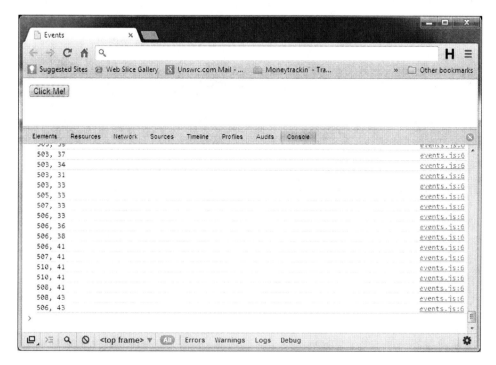

Figure 7.7. Logging mouse co-ordinates

Continuing the video game theme, suppose we wish to log user keystrokes. Firstly add a text area to your HTML page as follows:

```
<textarea id="myTextArea"></textarea>
```

Then, to avoid cluttering the console, remove the mouse logging code and replace it with the following:

```
var txtArea = document.getElementById("myTextArea");

txtArea.onkeypress = function(e) {
  console.log(String.fromCharCode(e.keyCode));
};
```

keyCode is a numerical representation of the pressed key. We use the built-in fromCharCode function to convert from a number to the actual key pressed. When you start typing into the text area, you should see something similar to Figure 7.8.

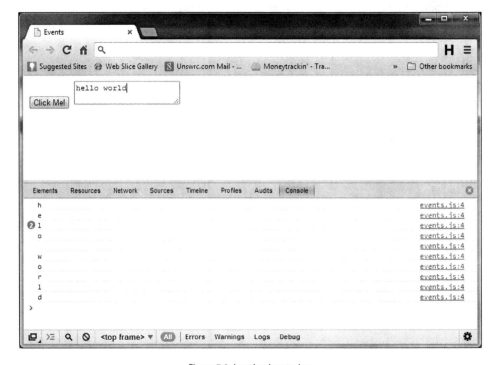

Figure 7.8. Logging keystrokes

You now know enough about JavaScript events to handle a wide variety of situations within your own application. However, suppose we want our events to interoperate with other code. Does JavaScript provide a mechanism to facilitate this? The answer is yes, and we will address this in the next section.

Custom Events

JavaScript provides a simple mechanism for creating custom events. Before describing the details of the implementation, it is worth going over an example use case, since the use of custom events is not always obvious to someone new to JavaScript. Suppose our to-do application is complete, but somebody else wishes to write a plugin to display a fancy notification to the user every time they add a new item to their list.

How should they go about doing this? One possible option would be for the other programmer to modify our script and place their notification code inside ours. This is problematic on several fronts. Firstly, they may not have access to our source code. Although JavaScript will always be viewable as plain text, before shipping, we may choose to compress our code to improve loading times. This would make our source code very difficult to work with directly.

But what if we granted access to our original source code? Directly altering the to-do list code base is still a bad idea for a number of reasons. Firstly, if we decide to update our to-do list code, it may break the other programmer's modification. Secondly, if a number of programmers all wish to create their own plugins, the original code base will quickly become bloated and unmanageable.

The problem with the above solution is that it involves modifying our to-do list code to incorporate functionality that it does not need to know anything about. While the plugin code needs to know about the to-do list, the reverse is not true: The to-do list application does not need to know about any plugins. In theory, it should be possible for thousands of plugins to be written while our original program happily chugs along in ignorant bliss. The technical term for this architecture is loose coupling. Let's now make this concept a little less abstract by providing an actual implementation using a custom event.

A custom event can be created by using the following general construct:

```
var event = new CustomEvent(type, eventInitDict);
```

Here, `type` is the name of the custom event, and is something we define. `eventInitDict` provides the initialization parameters.

`eventInitDict` is itself a JavaScript object that takes the following three parameters:

bubbles   A Boolean indicating whether the event bubbles up through the DOM or not. The bubble phase and capture phase were covered earlier in this chapter.

cancelable   A Boolean indicating whether the event is cancelable. If an event is cancelable it means that it can have its default action prevented.

detail   The data passed when initializing the event. We will populate this object depending upon what data we wish to transmit with our custom event.

Let's use an example to illustrate the above. Create a new file named **customevent.html** containing the following HTML:

```
<!doctype html>
<html>
<head>
  <title>Events</title>
</head>
<body>
  <button id="btnAdd">Add Task</button>
  <script src="customevent.js"></script>
</body>
</html>
```

This represents our dummy to-do list application. Next, create a file named **customevent.js** containing the following JavaScript code:

```
var taskEvent = new CustomEvent("TaskAdded", {
  detail: {
    message: "A task has been added",
  },
  bubbles: true,
  cancelable: true
});
var btnAdd = document.getElementById("btnAdd");

btnAdd.onclick = function(e) {
  document.dispatchEvent(taskEvent);
};
```

The above code creates a custom event. We define the name to be `"TaskAdded"` and then provide the event with the initialization parameters. Every time the button is clicked, we use `dispatchEvent` to trigger the event. Our event can now be handled in exactly the same way as native events such as keystrokes and mouse clicks. We make the simplifying assumption that a task is added every time the button is clicked. In a real application you would likely only fire the event if all the error checking passed. So now we have a mockup of a very simple application; all it does is trigger a custom event when the button is clicked. Suppose somebody now wishes to write a plugin: Add the following code to a new file named **customeventplugin.js**:

```
function handleTaskAdded(e) {
    alert(e.detail.message);
}

document.addEventListener("TaskAdded", handleTaskAdded, false);
```

Add the following line to **customevent.html**:

```
<script src="customeventplugin.js"></script>
```

When you refresh the page and click on the button you should now see a sight such as shown in Figure 7.9.

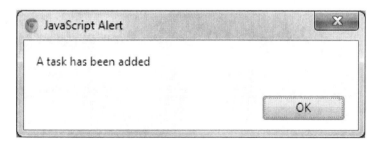

Figure 7.9. Using custom events

The use of custom events has some powerful implications. If we have a well-designed event API, it means that other libraries and code bases can now interoperate with our code purely by responding to events. These other code bases never directly need to access our source code. A custom event can be triggered in any number of situations, it does not just have to be a user-generated event. This mechanism opens up the possibility of creating rich JavaScript ecosystems by way of interacting loosely coupled components. Let's turn to how we use events in our project.

Project

Adding Tasks

Our to-do list application needs to deal with and respond to a number of user events. Users add a task by submitting a form. This is handled in JavaScript as follows:

```
addForm.onsubmit = function(e) {
  var val;

  preventDefault(e);
  val = newTaskField.value;

  if (val === "") {
    warn("Please enter a task");
  } else {
    newTaskField.value = "";
    clearWarning();
    addTask(val);
  }
};
```

First we add the `onsubmit` handler to detect when a user has submitted the form. We use `preventDefault` to prevent the default action because we do not want the form to actually be submitted to a server!

 Preventing Default Actions

Some HTML elements have default actions. For example, forms are submitted, anchors follow hyperlinks, and checkboxes are toggled. By default, JavaScript does not inhibit these default actions. In other words, if you fire an event when a user clicks an anchor, your event handler will be called, but the browser will also continue with the standard action by following the hyperlink. If this is undesirable behavior based on your application's needs, the event's `preventDefault` method can be used to tell the browser to stop the default action from occurring.

In our example, we check for an empty task, at which point we display a warning. If the task is valid, we clear any prior warnings and then add the task to the list.

Sorting

When our user wishes to sort items, they click on one of 'Name', 'Priority Low To High', or 'Priority High To Low', as seen in Figure 7.10.

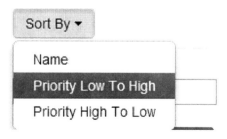

Figure 7.10. The sort menu for our app

In the HTML these text values have been defined as anchor tags. We have already retrieved the tags with the following code:

```
sortByLowHighAnchor = document.getElementById("sortByLowHigh");
sortByHighLowAnchor = document.getElementById("sortByHighLow");
sortByNameAnchor = document.getElementById("sortByName");
```

In Chapter 4 we wrote the actual sorting code. Now we can glue these pieces together with event handlers as follows:

```
sortByLowHighAnchor.onclick = function(e) {
  preventDefault(e);
  tasks = sortByLowHigh(tasks);
  renderTaskList();
};

sortByHighLowAnchor.onclick = function(e) {
  preventDefault(e);
  tasks = sortByHighLow(tasks);
  renderTaskList();
};

// Sort tasks by name
sortByNameAnchor.onclick = function(e) {
  preventDefault(e);
  tasks = sortByName(tasks);
  renderTaskList();
};
```

As before, we prevent the default action because we do not wish the browser to follow the actual link. Then we call our sorting function. Lastly we render the list with the new ordering.

Task Modification

Next we handle the processing of individual tasks. This function is slightly more involved because we need to keep track of which task is being actioned, along with which action is being performed. Add the following code to **todo.js**:

```
taskListForm.onclick = function(e) {
  var target, idx, targetClass;

  preventDefault(e);
  target = getTarget(e);
  idx = getIndex(target);

  if (idx) {
    idx = Number(idx);
    targetClass = target.getAttribute('class');

    if (targetClass === 'highpriority' || targetClass ===
'lowpriority' || targetClass === 'normalpriority') {
      setPriority(idx, target.getAttribute("value"));
    } else if (target.className.match("delete-task")) {
      removeTask(idx);
    } else if (target.type === "checkbox") {
      toggleComplete(idx);
    }
  }
};
```

Firstly, we retrieve the index of the item and store it into the variable `idx`. If this is a valid value, we take the class of the HTML element and store it in the variable `targetClass`. We then test for three separate cases. In the first case, `targetClass` indicates the user has clicked on priority sorting. In this case. we retrieve the value of the HTML element and use this number to set the priority of the task. In the second case, `targetClass` indicates that the user has clicked on delete. In this case we can simply remove the item. In third and final case, the user has clicked on a checkbox, at which point we know to toggle whether or not the task of been completed. This completes our exploration of event handling.

Summary

We have covered the main aspects of JavaScript event handling in this chapter. We began by describing DOM events, specifically what constitutes an event and where to find a list of events. We then took a technical detour to cover propagation, the path that an event takes to get from the user to your application. Next we explored assigning handlers. This is how HTML elements register for events and how functions are defined to handle a given event. From within an event handler, we then learned how to find out about HTML elements and get event object information. We also discussed custom events, discovering how to get your application to fire its own internally defined event.

Chapter **8**

Canvas

This chapter introduces the <canvas> element, which is part of the HTML5 specification. We'll be using <canvas> to implement a productivity chart for our example application. The chart will update each time the data is changed. This will show the user how many tasks have been completed and how many remain unfinished. We'll also add some shadowing and gradient effects to give our charts a more polished look.

What is Canvas?

The official specification[1] states: "The canvas element provides scripts with a resolution-dependent bitmap canvas, which can be used for rendering graphs, game graphics, art, or other visual images on the fly." Although the specification does not mandate an actual scripting language, JavaScript is generally the language used.

---

[1] http://www.whatwg.org/specs/web-apps/current-work/multipage/the-canvas-element.html#the-canvas-element

Canvas Versus SVG

The material in this chapter could have also been written using **Scalable Vector Graphics** (SVG). SVG is a language for describing two-dimensional graphics in XML. Both Canvas and SVG have widespread adoption; each has its own strengths and weaknesses[2]. In the end, we chose Canvas for the practical reason that it is JavaScript-based. For those curious to explore SVG, the Mozilla Developer Network has both documentation and examples.[3]

We can provide a basic canvas for our users:

```html
<div align="center">
  <br /><br />
  <h2>Productivity Chart</h2>
  <canvas id="canvas" height="300" width="400">
  </canvas>
</div>
```

Place this code in **index.html** just before `<ul class="template">`. A basic canvas can be provided by using the `<canvas>` tag. We also specify an `id`, a height, and a width for the canvas. If no values are provided, or if the values provided cannot be correctly parsed, the default values are used: 300 for the width and 150 for the height. It is possible for a page to have multiple `<canvas>` elements, but for this project we'll just be using one. Our code will provide, pardon the pun, a blank canvas, with no content.

Our first task is to cater to those browsers without support for the `<canvas>` element. As of the time of writing, the canvas element is supported in 85% of browsers[4]. All modern major browsers, including those on mobile devices, support the `<canvas>` element. Although listed as unsupported, IE8 can actually support `<canvas>` functionality if developers wish to add one additional `<script>` tag to use a third-party library.[5]

---

[2] http://dev.opera.com/articles/view/svg-or-canvas-choosing-between-the-two/

[3] https://developer.mozilla.org/en-US/docs/SVG

[4] http://caniuse.com/#feat=canvas

[5] https://code.google.com/p/explorercanvas/

With IE8 included, browser support would jump to a very healthy 95%. For those browsers without support for <canvas>, it is easy to provide fallback content. We can place fallback content between the <canvas> and </canvas> tags as follows:

```
<canvas id="canvas" height="300" width="400">
  To Do:<div id="numToDo"></div>
  Done:<div id="numDone"></div>
</canvas>
```

For now, we provide some blank placeholders. When we render our chart, we'll update the fallback content to display the actual number of tasks completed, as well as the number of tasks to go.

Preparing the Data

Let's perform some basic computations around the number of tasks completed and the number of tasks remaining. Add the following function to **todo.js**:

```
function renderChart(tasks) {
    var done = countComplete(tasks);
    var todo = tasks.length - done;

    document.getElementById("numToDo").innerHTML = todo;
    document.getElementById("numDone").innerHTML = done;

    var dataValue = [todo, done];
    var maxVal = todo > done ? todo : done;
}
```

First, we establish the number of tasks completed by using our previously written countComplete function. By inference, we can calculate the number of tasks to do by taking the total number of tasks and subtracting the number of tasks completed. We then update our fallback content with these values for browsers not supporting <canvas>. We then put the values into an array, which will make it easier to use with our graph. Finally, we compute the maximum value, which will determine the largest number for our y-axis. This is calculated by taking the larger of the number of tasks completed and the number of tasks yet to do.

Setting up the Canvas

With the computations complete, we need a few lines of code to prepare the canvas for drawing. Continuing on, we add the following code:

```
var topMargin = 25;
var bottomMargin = 1;
var canvas = document.getElementById("canvas");

canvas.width = canvas.width;
```

We specify, in pixels, the margin of the chart from the top and bottom of the canvas. This margin is unrelated to any of the built-in variables. It is a variable that we're declaring, and we will use it to do some computations and canvas scaling later. Then, we retrieve the actual `<canvas>` element using `document.getElementById`. The following line of code may initially appear puzzling:

```
canvas.width = canvas.width;
```

To make sense of it, we refer to the specification,[6] which states: "When the canvas element is created, and subsequently whenever the width and height attributes are set (whether to a new value or to the previous value), the bitmap and any associated contexts must be cleared back to their initial state and re-initialized with the newly specified coordinate space dimensions."

In other words, whenever the height or width is changed, the canvas is reset. We take advantage of this behavior, and reset the canvas before doing any drawing to make sure that any old data is erased.

 The Official Specification

Astute readers may notice that we have so far referred to two different *official* specifications. Historically, the Web Hypertext Application Technology Working Group (WHATWG) began working on a new HTML specification while the World Wide Web Consortium (W3C) was focusing on XHTML. Ultimately, XHTML was abandoned, and the two groups are now working together on HTML5. This has left us with two different, but largely compatible, specifications. From the view

---

[6] http://www.w3.org/TR/2010/WD-html5-20101019/the-canvas-element.html

of an application developer, both can be treated as authoritative sources. Minor differences are likely to only come to the fore if one wished to undertake the task of writing an HTML5 parser or similar.

The Most Basic Drawing

Before we do any drawing, we check to make sure that the browser supports the `canvas` object. Continuing on from our previous examples:

```
if (canvas && canvas.getContext) {
}
```

This contains a subtlety that is worth exploring. Notice how we use `canvas.getContext` instead of `canvas.getContext()`. The difference can be illustrated with this example:

```
function testFunction() {
  return 0
}

if (testFunction()) {
  console.log('with parentheses');
}

if (testFunction) {
  console.log('no parentheses');
}
```

Only `'no parentheses'` will print. The first `if` statement will call the function and evaluate its return value, but this is far from our aim. The second `if` statement will simply test if the function exists; this is exactly what we want to do. We need to make sure the `canvas` object has a `getContext` function; we want to avoid calling that function and evaluating its output!

Let's begin by establishing the context. Place the following code within the `if` statement:

```
var context = canvas.getContext("2d");
```

As we've checked that the `getContext` function exists, we can now actually call it. This function takes a single parameter, the context type. Currently, the canvas contexts that are available are "2d" and "webgl". The 2d context is defined as[7]: "The 2D context represents a flat Cartesian surface whose origin (0,0) is at the top-left corner, with the coordinate space having x values increasing when going right, and y values increasing when going down."

Basically, it's a flat surface that we can use for drawing. It's important to note that the origin is the top-left corner, and y values increase when going down. This is different from the more familiar Cartesian plane, which has y values increasing when moving up. Because our graph has y values increasing when going up in the more traditional fashion, we'll need to apply some transformations further on.

Note, also, that because of the way the default coordinate system is defined, negative coordinates aren't used. They will cause no errors, but they won't display on the screen. The other type of context, WebGL[8], is considered more experimental at this point than the 2d context, and is primarily used for rendering 3D graphics without the need for third-party plugins. We won't be exploring WebGL in this book.

You'll notice that, by default, the canvas displays with a light gray fill. Let's replace it with a white background to demonstrate some simple concepts:

```
context.fillStyle = '#FFFFFF';
context.fillRect(0, 0, canvas.width, canvas.height);
```

We're specifying a `fillStyle` of #FFFFFF, which is white. The `fillStyle` attribute represents the color or style to use inside shapes. Here we are using it to indicate a color; later on, we'll specify a gradient.

We then call the function `fillRect` to fill in a rectangle with the expressed color around the specified coordinates. `fillRect` takes four parameters: the x coordinate of the upper-left corner, the y coordinate of the upper-left corner, the width of the rectangle in pixels, and the height of the rectangle in pixels. If you refresh the page, you'll notice that the canvas is now completely white. Let's delineate our canvas with a black border:

---

[7] http://www.w3.org/html/wg/drafts/2dcontext/html5_canvas/
[8] http://en.wikipedia.org/wiki/WebGL

```
context.strokeStyle = '#000000';
context.strokeRect(0, 0, canvas.width, canvas.height);
```

The `strokeStyle` attribute represents the color or style to use for the lines around the shapes. Here, we set the `strokeStyle` to #000000, which is black, and then draw a line around specified coordinates. `strokeStyle` takes the same parameters as `fillRect`. The main difference is that it will draw the stated rectangle without actually filling it in with the chosen color. You should now have a white canvas surrounded by a black border.

Text and the Coordinate System

Let's now draw the text for the y-axis. This will help solidify our understanding of the canvas coordinate system. Add the following to **todo.js**:

```
var textX = 10;
var textY = 190;

context.fillStyle = '#000000';
context.save();
context.translate(textX, textY);
context.rotate(Math.PI * -90 / 180);
context.fillText('Tasks Complete', 0, 0);
context.restore();
```

Once again, we set `fillStyle`—this time to black to determine the text color. Let's look at `save` and `restore`. We plan to draw some vertical text onto the canvas, running along the y-axis, much like one would see in a traditional graph. By default, text is rendered horizontally. In order for the text to be vertical, we'll need to transform the coordinate system. This is where `save` and `restore` come in. `save` will save the current state of the context. After we perform our transformation and draw the text vertically, we can bring back the state by calling `restore`, so that text by default will continue to render horizontally as expected, as shown in Figure 8.1.

 ### Saving and Restoring Data Stacks

For those of you with greater familiarity with data structures, it's worth noting that `save` and `restore` are implemented using a stack. Thus, it is possible to save multiple states. Calling `save` actually pushes the canvas state onto the top of the stack, while calling `restore` will "pop" the most recently pushed state off the top of the stack.

For those unfamiliar with data structures, it may be helpful to use an example from the everyday world: a pancake stack. `save` would be analogous to putting another pancake on top of the stack; `restore` would be akin to removing a pancake from the top. Just like with a pancake stack, in a computer science stack, a single operation will only affect items at the top of the stack. Inserting and removing from the middle is possible, but it requires multiple steps.

Recall that, by default, the origin of the coordinate system is (0, 0). We'd prefer to avoid drawing text at (0, 0) because this will place text in the corner of our canvas. That's why we use `translate(x, y)`, which will make (x, y) the new origin. We are setting (10, 190) to be the starting point for drawing text. Because we want our text to be vertical, we call the `rotate` function. This function takes a parameter indicating the number of radians by which the coordinate system is rotated clockwise. You may recall from high school that pi radians are equivalent to 180 degrees. Here we're rotating the canvas 90 degrees counterclockwise so that our text will correctly run from bottom to top.

Finally, we can render the actual text by calling `fillText`. This function takes three parameters. The first parameter is the text to draw, and is followed by the x, y coordinates of the text, which we set to (0,0).

You may be wondering if we could have saved some work by just using `context.fillText('Tasks Complete', textX, textY)`. We can achieve the same result if we remove `translate` and alter `fillText` to:

```
context.fillText('Tasks Complete', -190, 10);
```

However, our slightly longer example helps us to avoid negative coordinates, and is more intuitive. Note that in the amended example, the y-coordinate of (-190) is actually in the spot where the x-coordinate would traditionally be, and vice-versa with the x-coordinate. This is because we're working with the rotated canvas, so the positions need to be swapped. A bit confusing, isn't it? The extra line of code is worth the increased clarity.

Figure 8.1. Y-axis text

A Further Rotation Example

Let's take a short break from the main project and look at a side example involving shapes. This is a useful exercise because shape rotation is visually more instructive and intuitive than text rotation. Create a new files named **canvas.html**:

```
                                                              canvas-1.html
<!doctype html>
<html>
<head>
  <title>Todo</title>
</head>
<body>
  <canvas id="canvas" height="300" width="400">
  </canvas>
```

```
    <script src="canvas.js"></script>
  </body>
</html>
```

Next, create **canvas.js**:

canvas-1.js

```
var canvas = document.getElementById("canvas");
var context = canvas.getContext("2d");

context.strokeStyle = '#000000';
context.strokeRect(0, 0, canvas.width, canvas.height);
context.fillRect(100, 100, 200, 100);
```

You should have a thin black line surrounding the canvas along with a solid black rectangle on the screen, as seen in Figure 8.2.

Figure 8.2. Drawing a solid black rectangle

Now add the following line of code immediately after `getContext`:

```
context.rotate(10 * Math.PI / 180);
```

Notice how the entire context is rotated 10 degrees clockwise. Switch the 10 to a
-10 and observe what happens. Now adjust the -10 to 45. Then, change the 45 to a
90 and observe how it rotates the context entirely off the screen save for a single
thin border. As a final experiment, move `context.rotate(90 * Math.PI / 180);`
to the very last line. Note that `rotate` has no effect on shapes and lines that have
already been rendered to the screen. Subsequent drawings will, of course, be rotated
as expected.

Y-axis Numbering

Let's return to the main project by adding some numbers to the y-axis. Before
moving on to this section, make sure that you have a few items in your list so that
some sensible numbers can be displayed on the graph. Add the following code to
todo.js after `context.restore()`:

```
        var yScaleFactor = (canvas.height - topMargin) / (maxVal);
        var count =  0;

        for (var yAxisValue = maxVal; yAxisValue >= 0;
➥yAxisValue -= 1) {
            var yCoord = topMargin - bottomMargin +
➥(yScaleFactor * count);

            context.fillText(yAxisValue, 40, yCoord);
            count++;
        }
```

The first task is to compute the y-axis scale factor. This variable represents the dis-
tance between two numbers on our y-axis. We compute it by taking the canvas
height, subtracting the top margin and then dividing by the maximum value of the
y-axis. The result will give us the appropriate spacing between each number.

Now we need to draw the numbers on the axis. You'll notice that the for loop starts
at the maximum value and then counts backwards. Recall that under the default
coordinate system, the top-left corner is (0, 0) and the Y-axis descends downwards
as y increases. Therefore, the smallest number on our Y-axis, being 0, will correspond
with the largest y-coordinate. Similarly, the largest number on the Y-axis will correspond with the smallest y-coordinate. If this is hard to grasp, I'd recommend paste
in the code and reread the explanation using the graph as a visual aid, and it should
become clearer. Figure 8.3 illustrates this point.

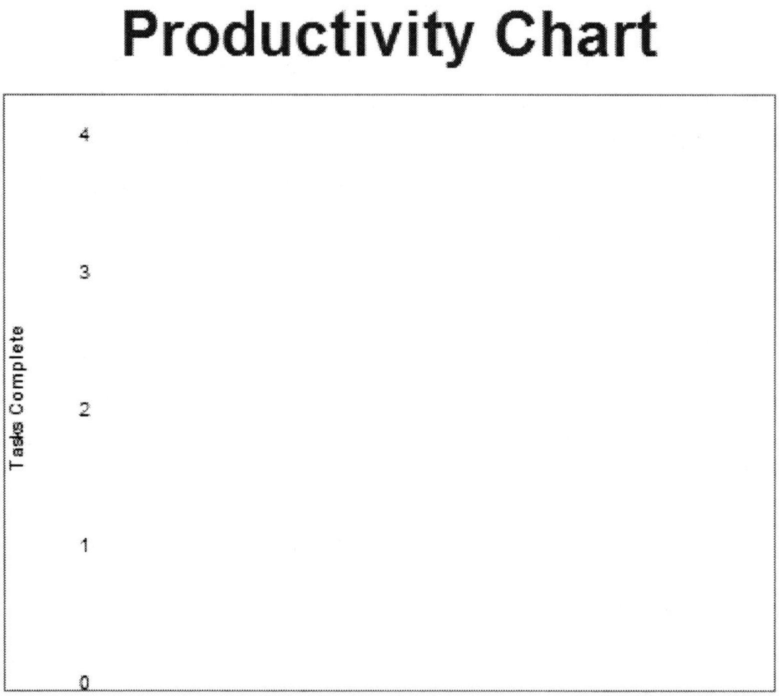
Productivity Chart
Tasks Complete
4
3
2
1
0

Figure 8.3. Numbered axis

We calculate the y-coordinate by subtracting the bottom margin from the top margin, then incrementing by `yScaleFactor` on each iteration of the `for` loop. We then call `fillText` as before to draw the text at the specified y-coordinate, 40 pixels in from the x-axis. Our graph is starting to take shape!

"Hello World" Canvas-style

Because text elements are merely decorations on the graph, let's look at another side example to gain a better understanding of some canvas text API features. Replace **canvas.js** from our prior example with the following:

canvas-2.js

```
var canvas = document.getElementById("canvas");
var context = canvas.getContext("2d");
var message = "Hello world";
var xCoord = canvas.width / 2;
```

```
        var yCoord = canvas.height / 2;

        context.font = "italic 30pt Times New Roman";
        context.fillStyle = "blue";
        context.textAlign = "center";
        context.textBaseline = "middle";
        context.fillText(message, xCoord, yCoord);
```

`context.font` can be used to set font properties. Here we specify a style, size, and font face. Change `fillText` to `strokeText` and observe what happens. Fill and stroke behave similarly for text as they do for shapes. There's also a function, `measureText`, that's available to measure the length of the rendered text. Add the following and then refresh your page:

```
        var metrics = context.measureText(message);
        var width = metrics.width;

        context.fillText( width + 'pixels', xCoord, yCoord + 70);
```

`measureText` returns the width of the text based on the provided text and the current font. There's no function for returning the height of text; the height of text in pixels is the same as the font size in points. In this case, the font height is 30 pixels.

Grid Lines

Heading back to the main project, let's draw some horizontal grid lines to make it easy to see the numerical value on the bar chart. Add the following two lines of code within our `for` loop:

```
        count++;


        context.moveTo(0, yCoord);
        context.lineTo(canvas.width, yCoord);
```

The `moveTo` function moves the cursor to the specified coordinate, while the `lineTo` function creates a line to the specified coordinate. At this point, nothing has actually been rendered to the screen. To do this, add these two lines after our `for` loop:

```
for (var yAxisValue = maxVal; scale >= 0; yAxisValue -= 1) {
  ...
}

context.lineWidth = 0.1;
context.stroke();
```

lineWidth specifies the width of a line in pixels. To make the line visible, we call the stroke function, which will finally render the paths to the screen, as shown in Figure 8.4

Figure 8.4. Grid lines

Rectangles

We will represent our column graph using rectangles, which are the only shapes that are natively supported. Although it is possible to draw shapes of arbitrary complexity, only rectangles have a specialized function. Before drawing the rectangles, we need to perform a few context manipulations. Following on from context.stroke(), insert:

```
var xScaleFactor = canvas.width / (dataValue.length + 1);

context.translate(0, canvas.height);
context.scale(xScaleFactor, -1 * yScaleFactor);
drawRect(context);
```

First, we create the xScaleFactor. Analogous to the yScaleFactor variable, this allows us to compute the spacing between columns. Recall that translate changes the origin of the coordinate system. Here, we're changing it from the top-left corner to the bottom-left corner, which will assist in drawing the columns.

scale is a built-in function that takes two parameters, x and y. Anything drawn subsequent to this function call is made bigger horizontally by x and bigger vertically by y. For example, if y is 3, everything drawn will be three times as tall. In this case, by applying a negative number we ensure that our rectangles start from the bottom of the graph and are drawn upwards. Without this, the rectangles will be drawn in the default downwards direction.

We can provide a function to draw our rectangles:

```
if (canvas && canvas.getContext) {
    ...
}


function drawRect(context) {
  for (i = 0; i < dataValue.length; i++) {
    var startX = i+1;
    var startY = bottomMargin / xScaleFactor;
    var endX = 1;
    var endY = dataValue[i];
    var width = 0.5;
    var gradient = context.createLinearGradient(startX,
➡startY, endX, endY);

    gradient.addColorStop(0.0, "#8ED6FF");
    gradient.addColorStop(1.0, "#004CB3");
    context.fillStyle = gradient;
    context.fillRect(startX, startY, width, endY);
  }
}
```

To draw the rectangles, we begin by looping through each value in our data set. In this case, there are only two values: the number of items to do and the number of items completed. Then we use the built-in `createLinearGradient` function, which takes four parameters. The first two parameters represent the x and y coordinates of the starting point of the gradient, while the latter two represent the gradient's endpoint. We're using this function to provide our column graph with a bit of texture, instead of a plain single-color column.

The `addColorStop` function helps define the colors and position of the gradient. The first parameter is a float between 0.0 and 1.0 representing the start and end point of a gradient. It is possible to add an arbitrary number of color stops. We've just added two stops, one at the beginning and one at the end. The second parameter represents the color. Here we transition from light to dark blue. Remember how previously we used `fillStyle` to define a color? Here we use it to define the gradient. Finally, we call `fillRect` as we've done before, as shown inFigure 8.5.

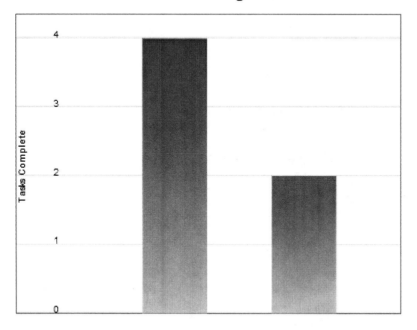

Figure 8.5. Our chart with drawn rectangles

Arcs

We've mentioned how rectangles are the only natively supported shape, but this does not indicate that shapes such as circles are unavailable. It just means there is no `fillCircle` or similar function. Let's explore how we might draw some non-rectangular shapes. Replace all of **canvas.js** with the following:

```
var canvas = document.getElementById("canvas");
var context = canvas.getContext("2d");

context.beginPath();
context.arc(50, 50, 50, 0, Math.PI, true);
context.stroke();
```

The only unfamiliar aspect of the above is the `arc` function. This takes five parameters, where the first two parameters represent the x and y coordinate of the circle's center. The third parameter is the radius of the circle, while the fourth and fifth parameters represent the start and end of the arc in radians. In this case, we start at 0, which is the same as the x-axis. By choosing `Math.PI` as the end angle, we are drawing a semicircle (pi radians is 180 degrees). The final task is to determine whether the circle is drawn clockwise or counterclockwise. This is specified by the last parameter, which we have set to `true`, indicating counterclockwise.

Many of the concepts you've learned from drawing rectangles can be applied to arcs. For instance, you can replace `stroke` with `fill`. So far, we've just been dealing with toy examples; you should look at some of the breathtaking examples of canvas in action[9].

Bar Chart Labels

Our charts will need some labels to indicate which columns represent tasks done and tasks still to do. Insert the following immediately after we define `xScaleFactor`, but before `translate`:

```
var dataName = ["To Do", "Done"];

context.textBaseline = "bottom";
```

---

[9] http://rectangleworld.com/blog/archives/462

```
for (i = 0; i < dataValue.length; i++) {
    var yCoord = canvas.height - dataValue[i] * yScaleFactor;

    context.fillText(dataName[i], xScaleFactor * (i + 1),
➥yCoord);
    }
```

We specify `textBaseLine` to position the vertical alignment of the text. If you scroll down to the bottom of http://www.html5tutorial.info/html5-canvas-text.php[10], you'll see a visual representation of the different types of alignment.

We then calculate the x- and y-coordinates so that the text will be positioned on top of the columns. We then render the text using `fillText` as earlier.

Shadows

For a nice finishing touch to our graph, we'll add some shadows to our columns. Add this code just before `drawRect(context)`:

```
context.shadowOffsetX = 2;
context.shadowOffsetY = 2;
context.shadowBlur = 2;
context.shadowColor = "rgba(0, 0, 0, 0.5)";
```

`shadowOffsetX` and `shadowOffsetX` specify the horizontal and vertical offset respectively, in pixels, to the shadow. `shadowBlur` is a parameter that uses an equation to determine how much the shadow should be blurred. `shadowColor` is used to indicate the color. Shadows can be applied to text, shapes, and images. As Figure 8.6 shows, the drawing of our graph is complete!

---

[10] http://www.html5tutorial.info/html5-canvas-text.php

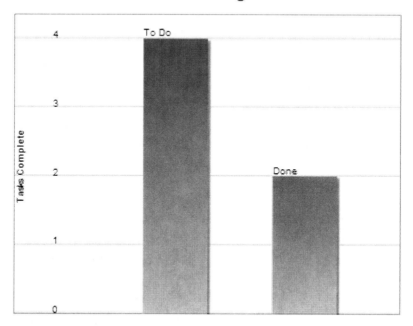

Figure 8.6. Finished chart

Making Images

Let's finish this chapter with a bit of fun, and give users the ability to convert their chart into an image. Perhaps they'll use it as inspirational wallpaper to get things done! Add the following to **index.html** just below the closing `<canvas>` tag:

```
<div class='row'>
  <a id='printChart' href='' class='btn'>Print Chart</a>
</div>
```

Now we just have to add one line of code to the bottom of the `renderChart` function:

```
document.getElementById('printChart').href = canvas.toDataURL();
```

`toDataUrl` is a built-in function that returns a URL with a representation of the image. It takes an optional parameter specifying the image type, of which the default is PNG. If you wish to specify image/jpeg, this function also takes a second parameter between 0.0 and 1.0 to indicate the image quality. When you refresh and click on the button, you'll be taken to an image that you'll be able to save.

Summary

Congratulations, you have achieved quite a lot in this chapter. We began with an introduction to the <canvas> element. Next, you learned how to draw text, rectangles, and lines using the canvas API. From there, we moved on to more advanced topics such as canvas rotation and scaling, gradients, and shadow effects. Finally, you learned how to save a canvas as an image file. Of course, throughout the entire chapter, you also learned how to create canvas based charts to work with the book's example project.

Now that you've read through this book, you should have a good grasp of the JavaScript programming language. Though the scope and size of this book didn't allow us to dive as deeply into the language as books many times the size of this one might, you should nonetheless have a good base to build on. You're guaranteed to use the fundamentals we've covered in whatever JavaScript program you end up writing, regardless of whether it's simple or extremely complex. Remember, this book sped you through JavaScript at a quick pace. You'll undoubtedly get to a point where you'll want to delve further into some of what we covered here, or other, more advanced topics that we didn't. Stay curious, ask questions and dig. At the rate the Web is evolving, there are practically no limits to what you can build.

Appendix A: Common Events

Here are some of the most commonly used JavaScript events.

Event Name	Event Type	Specification	Fired when...
abort	UIEvent	DOM L3	The loading of a resource has been aborted.
blur	FocusEvent	DOM L3	An element has lost focus (does not bubble).
click	MouseEvent	DOM L3	A pointing device button has been pressed and released on an element.
contextmenu	MouseEvent	DOM L3	The right button of the mouse is clicked (before the context menu is displayed).
dblclick	MouseEvent	DOM L3	A pointing device button is clicked twice on an element.
drag	DragEvent	HTML5	An element or text selection is being dragged (every 350ms).
dragend	DragEvent	HTML5	A drag operation is ending (by releasing a mouse button or hitting the escape key).

Event Name	Event Type	Specification	Fired when...
dragenter	DragEvent	HTML5	A dragged element or text selection enters a valid drop target.
dragleave	DragEvent	HTML5	A dragged element or text selection leaves a valid drop target.
dragover	DragEvent	HTML5	An element or text selection is being dragged over a valid drop target (every 350ms).
dragstart	DragEvent	HTML5	The user starts dragging an element or text selection.
drop	DragEvent	HTML5	An element is dropped on a valid drop target.
error	UIEvent	DOM L3	A resource failed to load.
focus	FocusEvent	DOM L3	An element has received focus (does not bubble).
hashchange	HashChangeEvent	HTML5	The fragment identifier of the URL has changed (the part of the URL after the #).
input	Event	HTML5	The value of an element changes, or the content of

Event Name	Event Type	Specification	Fired when...
			an element with the attribute `contenteditable` is modified.
invalid	Event	HTML5	A submissable element has been checked and doesn't satisfy its constraints.
keydown	KeyboardEvent	DOM L3	A key is pressed down.
keypress	KeyboardEvent	DOM L3	A key is pressed down that normally produces a character value.
keyup	KeyboardEvent	DOM L3	A key is released.
load	UIEvent	DOM L3	A resource and its dependent resources have finished loading.
mousedown	MouseEvent	DOM L3	A pointing device button (usually a mouse) is pressed on an element.
mouseenter	MouseEvent	DOM L3	A pointing device is moved onto the element that has the listener attached.
mouseleave	MouseEvent	DOM L3	A pointing device is moved off the element that has

Event Name	Event Type	Specification	Fired when...
			the listener attached.
mousemove	MouseEvent	DOM L3	A pointing device is moved over an element.
mouseout	MouseEvent	DOM L3	A pointing device is moved off the element that has the listener attached or off one of its children.
mouseover	MouseEvent	DOM L3	A pointing device is moved onto the element that has the listener attached or onto one of its children.
mouseup	MouseEvent	DOM L3	A pointing device button is released over an element.
offline	Event	HTML5 offline	The browser has lost access to the network.
online	Event	HTML5 offline	The browser has gained access to the network (but particular websites might be unreachable).
pagehide	PageTransitionEvent	HTML5	A session history entry is being traversed from.

Event Name	Event Type	Specification	Fired when...
pageshow	PageTransitionEvent	HTML5	A session history entry is being traversed to.
popstate	PopStateEvent	HTML5	A session history entry is being navigated to (in certain cases).
reset	HTMLEvents (DOM L2) or Event (HTML5)	DOM L2, HTML5	A form is reset.
resize	UIEvent	DOM L3	The document view has been resized.
scroll	UIEvent	DOM L3	The document view or an element has been scrolled.
select	UIEvent	DOM L3	Some text is being selected.
show	MouseEvent	HTML5	A `contextmenu` event was fired on/bubbled to an element that has a `contextmenu` attribute.
submit	HTMLEvents (DOM L2) or Event (HTML5)	DOM L2, HTML5	A form is submitted.
unload	UIEvent	DOM L3	The document or a dependent resource is being unloaded

CPSIA information can be obtained at www.ICGtesting.com
Printed in the USA
BVOW06s2232230713

326807BV00001B/1/P

9 780987 332189